# Danish Textile Prints

100 Years of Craft and Design

Kirsten Toftegaard

# Danish Textile Prints
## 100 Years of Craft and Design

Strandberg Publishing

# Contents

# Introduction

**Bitten Hegelund**
(b.1960)

**'Pleat Orange'**
Cotton, 2004

After an analogue sketching process, Bitten Hegelund uses digital tools to test her pattern ideas. She likes to explore the illusion of three-dimensionality and staggered lines as a pattern-forming element.

# Introduction

Textile printing is a method for aesthetically enhancing a woven textile with combinations of images and patterns, rhythm and repetition, tactility and texture, colours and light, two-dimensionality and illusions of three-dimensionality. The technical possibilities are endless, and there are no limits to the types of decorations that can be applied to the textile to achieve the artist's, maker's or designer's intended expression. The end result may be a one-off hand-printed textile, a unique experimental work of textile art or an industrial fabric.

Designmuseum Danmark has a large collection of printed textiles collected over the past century. This book is the first printed presentation of this impactful visual material, which spans art, crafts and design.

The world-renowned Danish interior design culture owes much of its characteristic identity to Danish textile printing, with Marie Gudme Leth, Helga Foght, Inge Ingetoft and Dorte Raaschou among its key practitioners. In addition to a playful use of colours and expressive repeated visual elements, textile printing also embraced notes of poetry and humour. The present book works as a companion to the exhibition *The Power of Print: 100 Years of Danish Textile Printing* shown at Designmuseum Danmark from May 2025 to the end of the year. The book explores the history of Danish design and adds new nuance to our understanding of a century of Danish textile printing. The broad scope and deep significance of textile printing is often overlooked and has not been fully included in previous presentations of Danish modernism.

A search for Danish textile printing in Designmuseum Danmark's database produces more than 600 hits. The museum has been in existence for about 130 years (initially as the Danish Museum of Decorative Art, later as the Danish Museum of Art & Design and from 2011, under its current name), and the first printed textiles

**Inge Ingetoft**
(1929–1996)

**'Congo'**
Cotton, 1953

Several of Inge Ingetoft's print designs
were produced by L.F. Fogt. The monochrome print is broken up by thin,
abstract line drawings in the original
colour of the fabric.

were added to the collection in 1935. A more focused collection effort did not begin until the 1950s.

The two pieces purchased in 1935 were designed and printed by one of the pioneers of the field, textile printer Marie Gudme Leth. They were bought from Selskabet til Haandarbejdets Fremme (Danish Handcraft Guild) by the museum director, Vilhelm Slomann, who had a keen interest in textiles. During the 1930s and 1940s, only a few pieces were added to the collection, even though the profession had by then gained recognition among professional makers and artisans. Danish printed textiles appeared both in specialized exhibitions and in joint exhibitions alongside other Danish crafts and design objects, and textile printers were featured in crafts journals. It would take a few decades from the resumption of textile printing in Denmark until the museum realized its significance in Danish interior design culture.

The limited interest in the field at the Museum of Decorative Art is also reflected in the number of exhibitions dedicated to printed textiles. Until 1980, these can be counted on one hand. However, textile printers were included in group exhibitions at the museum arranged by Haandarbejdets Fremme and the Danish Society for Arts and Crafts. The first textile printer to hold a solo exhibition was Ruth Hull, who presented her work at the museum in spring 1971.

The textile print collection at Designmuseum Danmark represents about 80 designers. Naturally, the collection is far from exhaustive – when is any collection ever? – and textile printing afficionados will no doubt be able to spot individual textile printers or particular textiles that are missing. Due to the textiles' colourful patterns and because they could be laundered and ironed, they have been loved, used, reused, altered and worn to shreds. Thus, some patterns are known only from newspapers, magazines, journals and photographs.

**Ruth Hull**
(1912–1996)

**Checkered length of fabric**
Cotton, 1951

Ruth Hull liked to experiment with alternative printing elements. Here, she used long rods wrapped in felt that absorbed the ink. Her work also considered the effects of light in a room.

Throughout the 20th century, textile printing was mainly practised as a workshop industry by highly skilled makers. Most enterprises were small one-woman textile printing studios. This is a general characteristic of high-quality Danish textile art, textile printing and weaving, most of which was the work of small studios. This practice had its pros and cons. One drawback was that it often made it difficult to earn a living because of the limited scale of production. One advantage, on the other hand, was that it allowed for a high degree of experimentation, in part aimed at optimizing production – much higher than in the other Nordic countries, for example, where artists designed the patterns and left production to industry.

**Bodil Oxenvad**
(1915–2011)

**Sampler with hens**
Cotton, 1945

Bodil Oxenvad graduated from the School of Arts and Crafts in Copenhagen in 1946 but had her own studio from as early as 1942 until 1954, when she went to the United States. In Denmark, she created print designs for the retailers Magasin du Nord, Illum, Illums Bolighus and Fonnesbech.

**Grete Ehs Østergaard**
(b.1938)

**'Philodendron'**
Cotton, 1979

This length of fabric is based on a basic pattern of the same name. It is a one-off sample in which Grete Ehs Øster-gaard experimented with overprinting a cardiogram motif.

**Arne Jacobsen**
(1902–1971)

**'Havet' /**
**'The Sea'**
for Textil-Lassen
Cotton, 1950–1960

'Havet' was
printed in several
colourways.

Since textile printing was resumed as a decorative art during the late 1920s, it has remained largely a female profession, even to this day. As a result, the book focuses on women textile printers, including Helga Foght, Ruth Hull, Inge Ingetoft, Marie Gudme Leth, Dorte Raaschou and Grete Ehs Østergaard. More recent works are represented by Lisbeth Friis, Anne Fabricius Møller, Margrethe Odgaard, Vibeke Riisberg, Vibeke Rohland and Louise Sass, among others. Most of the men who designed prints for production were architects, graphic designers, painters and product designers, among them Arne Jacobsen, Axel Salto and Ole Kortzau. A common characteristic of textile print designers from other fields was that they did not own a textile printing workshop and were not personally involved in the printing process. With the exception of a few men who were trained textile printers, such as Rolf Middelboe and Hans Christian Rasmussen, women were the only ones who worked hands-on in the workshop.

It is hard not to suspect that the reason for the field's neglected status in Danish design history is that it was – and remains – a female profession.

These reservations aside, this book celebrates the makers and artists who created the printed textiles, the varying styles of patterns and colours and the development of Danish textile printing over the past one hundred years.

**Hans Christian Rasmussen**
(b.1949)

**'Blå Kant' / 'Blue Edge'**
Cotton, 1983

'Blå Kant' was made using screen printing, painting and spray technique. The textile was bought from the 1983 *Å-udstillingen* (The Å Exhibition), which was shown in Aarhus, Aabenraa and Aalborg.

# What is a pattern?

A motif consists of shapes, colours and intervals in between the shapes. If the motif or ornament is repeated in a template, it forms a pattern. This rhythmic repetition is called a pattern repeat. The repeat creates the pattern's inner tension.

In textiles, the pattern may arise during the weaving process, in which the threads intersect at right angles. The pattern may be generated by the structure of the weave, for example with a vertical, horizontal or diagonal design. It may also be applied to the fabric after weaving, for example in the form of textile printing or embroidery.

## Composition

Textile patterns are inherently two-dimensional and cover a flat surface, but an illusion of three-dimensionality can be achieved by altering the relationship of scale between shapes and intervals. Another key compositional feature is the deliberate use of colours, including contrasts and brightness. Minor adjustments can often change the character of the pattern. Altering the relative position of pattern elements gives rise to new patterns and rhythms. This can occur in a simple striped pattern as well as in a complicated organic pattern.

The principles of image composition apply to both the individual image in visual art and the recurring motif of a pattern.

## Stripes and checks

Stripes and checks were some of the first patterns that our ancestors used to decorate their textiles. These patterns are created during weaving. Stripes may follow the vertical yarns on the loom, the so-called warp, or they may be created by adding a different colour to the monochrome horizontal weft. When warp and weft stripes are combined, the result is a chequered textile. Most cultures have created woven or printed striped and chequered textiles, but since the width of the individual stripes – both vertical and horizontal – and of the intervals between them can be varied endlessly, no two striped or chequered textiles are ever quite the same.

## Organic patterns

Nature has always been an important source of inspiration. In the Western world, the significance has been mainly aesthetic, but in cultures living in close connection with nature, representations of animals and plants may carry religious, ritual and symbolic meaning.

## Geometric patterns

Geometric patterns adhere closely to the horizontal, vertical or diagonal structure of the weave.

The most common two-dimensional figures in geometric patterns are circle, triangle, square, rectangle, trapezoid, oval and ellipse. The most common three-dimensional forms are the sphere and the cone.

## Graphic patterns

Graphic patterns have a simple expression. They arise through compositions using colour contrasts, either between light and dark colours or between opposite colours on the colour circle. The colour circle is a model showing pure colours and their contrasting, or complementary, colours. Placed side by side, a colour and its complementary colour mutually intensify each other and produce a dynamic, sometimes vibrant expression.

## Hybrid patterns

Some patterns are more difficult to categorize and cannot be placed into any single group. They mix elements from different types of patterns – geometric and organic, realistic and stylized, recognizable and unrecognizable. Over time, these mixed patterns have been given a variety of labels, including 'bizarre' or 'surrealistic'. Today, they are often described as 'sampled' or 'hybrid' patterns.

# The principles of a pattern repeat

In a small repeat, the pattern consists of small recurring elements. The pattern may cover the full width of the fabric with a motif that is only repeated vertically.

The composition of the repeat affects the dynamic character of the pattern. The simplest method is to repeat the motif by laying out the repeat in horizontal and vertical directions.

An ornament may also be mirrored around a symmetry axis. Both methods produce static and stationary patterns, an effect that may be counteracted by the use of complex pattern elements.

A higher degree of internal tension in a pattern repeat can be achieved by including displacement, rotation and mirroring in the design. Such a shift may produce rhythmically expanding or wavy lines that automatically draw the eye. In some complicated patterns, the repeat can be difficult to discern, but the rhythm of the pattern is experienced both visually and physically.

Small pattern repeat with the motif repeated horizontally and vertically.

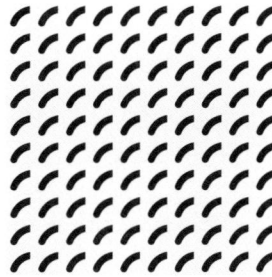

Horizontal and vertical pattern repeat.

Pattern repeat achieved by mirroring the motif horizontally and vertically.

Pattern repeat achieved by mirroring and rotating the motif horizontally and vertically.

Large pattern repeat, covering the full width of the fabric, with the motif repeated vertically.

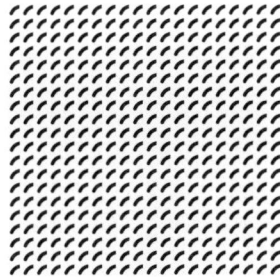

Pattern repeat staggered vertically by 50%.

Pattern repeat staggered horizontally by 50%.

Pattern repeat staggered vertically by 25%.

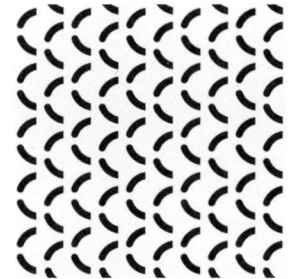

Pattern repeat staggered vertically by 50% and rotated (horizontal mirroring).

# Pioneers

**Ebbe Sadolin**
(1900–1982)

**Mana von Hausen Sadolin**
(1898–1993)

**Two wall panels with
scenes from mythology**
Cotton, 1925

Ebbe Sadolin's main practice was as
an illustrator – including for books
where he was also the author – and
as a designer for the Bing & Grøndahl
porcelain factory. During the 1920s,
he and his wife created batik prints,
including for wall panels that
were featured at the International
Exhibition of Modern Decorative
and Industrial Arts in 1925 in Paris
alongside furniture designed by the
architect Aage Rafn (1890–1953).

# Pioneers

During the early part of the 20th century, Denmark did not have an independent and creative textile printing profession. Most textile print patterns for home design and fashion were imported, often from France, Britain and Germany. The craft itself was all but forgotten in Denmark. Textile printing was originally part of the dyer's trade. In the 19th century, before industrialization transformed Denmark, many households wove their own textiles, which were dyed at a dyeing mill in the nearest market town.

For a brief period from 1916, one dyer, Einar Hansen in Vejle, printed textiles using his own hand-carved printing blocks. He took over his father's dyeing mill in 1918, and at the International Exhibition of Modern Decorative and Industrial Arts in 1925 in Paris, he won a gold medal for his printed textiles. Einar Hansen had in-depth scientific and technical knowledge about dyestuffs and their uses. Today, he is remembered mostly for his long, engaged collaboration with Danish weavers to develop subtle colour shades for dyeing yarns.

During the early decades of the 20th century, various artists took on batik printing. Batik, which originated in Asia, is a resistance printing technique, where part of the fabric is covered in hot, liquid wax, usually on both sides. The wax is applied with a brush, a printing block or the penlike tjanting tool. When the applied wax has dried, the fabric is submerged in a dye bath. Excess dye is rinsed out, and the wax is removed. The areas covered by wax resist the dye and remain the original colour of the fabric. For multi-colour pattern designs, the process is repeated for each colour. Batik can be categorized as a form of pattern dyeing. Batik dyeing is both laborious and time-consuming, and there are no shortcuts to a beautiful result.

Around 1900, the technique spread from Indonesia to Europe through the Netherlands. The impact on European decorative art was part of the oriental influence that washed over the arts in much of Europe during the late 19th century. Batik was perfectly aligned with Art Nouveau and its fascination with fluid lines and exotic expressions. The handmade batik prints also met the call for one-off works of decorative art, in line with the revival of European arts and crafts in opposition to industrial mass production. The popularity of batik peaked between 1920 and 1925. The art form had many practitioners, including many amateurs.

The technique was not suited for yard goods but found its way into interior decoration in the form of tablecloths, cushions, screens and lampshades. Silk batik was the highest fashion for clothing and accessories, including dresses, shawls or small handkerchiefs. The ornamentation was perfect for the 'Oriental' expression pursued by the leading fashion designer Paul Poiret, whose style was inspired by the ballet company Ballets Russes. It was also well suited for the *garçonne* style of the 1920s, with loose, narrow dresses and scarves with long tassels that moved in time with the modern music and lively dance steps of the time.

In spring 1924, the Finnish painter Mana von Hausen, who later marred the illustrator and ceramic artist Ebbe Sadolin, presented batik in the gallery Kunstboden in Hyskenstræde in Copenhagen, where she also demonstrated the technique to the public. A year and a half later, in September 1925, she again exhibited in Kunstboden, this time with Ebbe Sadolin. Mana von Hausen Sadolin showed furnishing fabrics as well as fabrics for clothing, such as shawls, scarves and dresses. All her works featured animals and flowers in multiple colours, while Ebbe Sadolin presented wall-hung textiles, screens and lampshades, many of them monochrome. He aimed for a simpler expression with landscapes and figures inspired by Greek, Mycenaean and African art.

Both Mana von Hausen Sadolin and Ebbe Sadolin were represented in the Danish pavilion at the International Exhibition of Modern Decorative and Industrial Arts in 1925 in Paris. Ebbe Sadolin's works in this exhibition were batik wall panels in reddish-brown tones for an interior with furniture designed by architect Aage Rafn and made by master cabinetmaker Otto Meyer. The wall panels, a peak example of Danish batik, attracted attention and were regarded as an exceptionally successful use of textile as wall decoration. Today, several of the wall panels – albeit it somewhat faded – are included in the collection at Designmuseum Danmark.

Ebbe Sadolin and Mana von Hausen Sadolin were awarded a Grand Prix for their works. Reportedly, they received the honour as a team. Thus, it is unclear whether Mana von Hausen Sadolin helped create the wall panels for the room with Aage Rafn's furniture or whether she received a Grand Prix for her own batik pieces. In any case, both artists received attribution for the wall panels when they were added to the museum's collection. In Paris, the painter Lissen Ewald, daughter of the Danish novelist Carl Ewald, presented a batik scarf, which is also included in the museum's collection.

The batik fever spread throughout much of Europe, but during the years after the 1925 Paris exhibition, the interest in the technique faded and eventually dissipated over the course of the 1930s. The time-consuming method, which was not well suited for the cool Danish climate, inevitably made batik a luxury item. Both Gudrun Stig Aagaard and Karen Schrader, who later became known for their textile printing, experimented with batik.

The industrial mass production of the 19th century had resulted in a large volume of cheap imported printed fabrics of poor quality. During the 1920s, the trend moved towards a simpler expression, with high

**Lissen Ewald**
(1890–1957)

**Batik scarf**
Silk, 1930

Lissen Ewald trained as a painter at the Royal Danish Academy of Fine Arts. Her practice included both paintings and crafts objects.

**Dorte Raaschou**
(1929–2011)

**'Blå Fisk' / 'Blue Fish'**
Silk organza, 1963

This printed fabric was bought from an
exhibition at Den Permanente in 1963.
It was designed for clothing.

demand for affordable, quality everyday products, including textiles, that met aesthetic as well as functional requirements. In the Nordic countries in particular, there was a desire to create products that would reach a wider part of the population. The prevailing trend was not about luxury products for the few but about elevating the quality of utilitarian objects for ordinary consumers.

In a sense, textile printing has always had a social aspect. Throughout much of its European history, textile printing has imitated complicated and precious weaves, as a much cheaper and simpler way to achieve the desired expression. This enabled a much wider audience to decorate their homes with patterned and colourful fabrics.

Textile printing enjoyed a revival during the 18th century driven by the large export of cotton fabrics from India to large parts of the world, including Europe. The Indian technique was quite elaborate, including techniques such as painting and block printing, a variety of substances and up to several successive dye baths, and it produced colourful, brilliant, vibrant patterns. Like batik, this technique too can be categorized as a form of pattern dyeing. European manufacturers tried to replicate and learn the technique and establish a domestic production. Used for clothing, the Indian cotton fabrics became at least as popular as precious silk fabrics. In response, many countries, including Denmark, banned the import of the colourful Indian cotton fabrics for many years.

Block printing is one of the oldest manual printing methods for transferring a pattern to textile or paper. It is a form of relief printing, where the image is defined by the raised areas that remain after the rest has been cut away. The dye is applied by pushing the block into a printing pad with an even distribution of dye. This transfers the dye to the raised areas of the block, which form the image. Next, the dye is transferred from the relief to the distended fabric. For multi-colour patterns, each colour is printed with a separate carved block.

Hardwood, including pearwood, walnut or boxwood, is the best choice for wooden printing blocks. A block may consist of multiple layers, with each layer

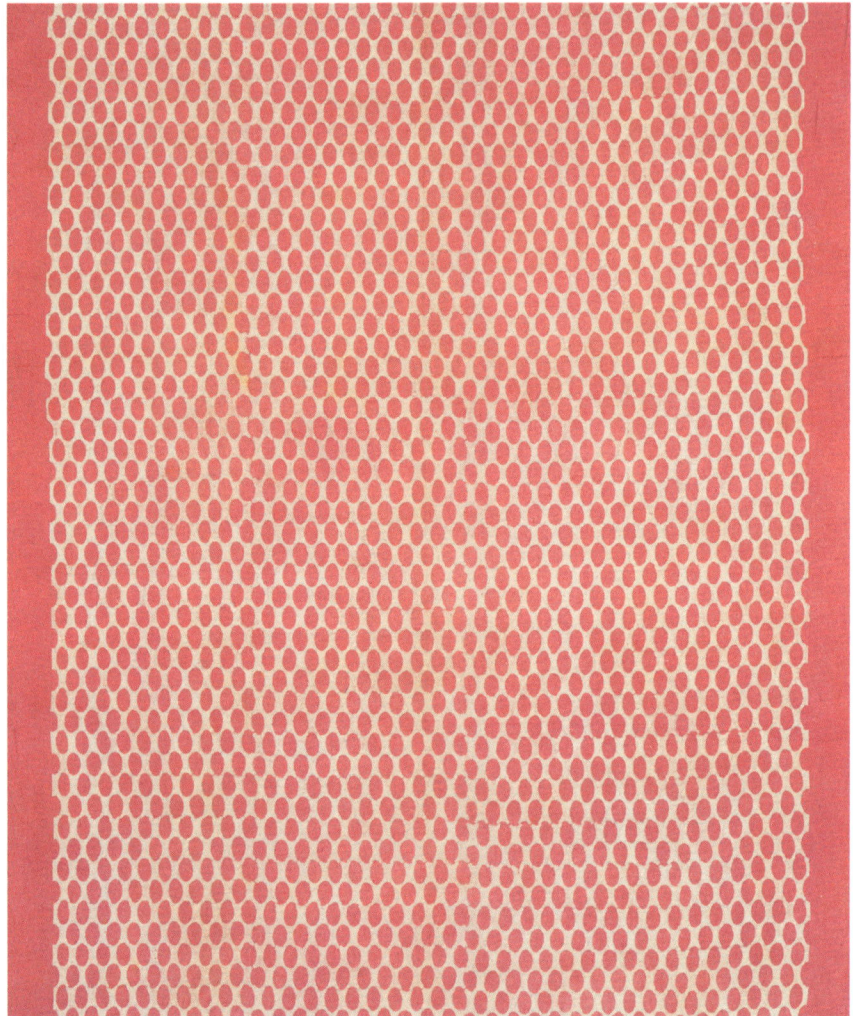

**Ingermarie Ostenfeld**
(1905–1998)

**Dressmaking fabric**
Cotton, 1940–1950

Ingermarie Ostenfeld trained with Marie Gudme Leth in 1935 before attending the Baden State Art School in Karlsruhe in 1938–1939. She established her own studio as early as 1936. She taught at the School of Arts and Crafts in Copenhagen from 1948 to 1949. Ingermarie Ostenfeld practised block printing, often as resist printing.

**Helga Foght**
(1902–1974)

**Length of fabric**
Linen, 1946–1955

For some time, Helga Foght worked with stylized nature themes, as in this untitled print.

rotated so that the wood grain runs crosswise to the adjacent layers. This makes the block stronger. Hardwood can withstand the many hammer strokes that repeated printing requires. 'Pounding and hammering, hammering and pounding, until you got a headache' – this was how Marie Gudme Leth described what it was like to be in a room during block printing, in a comment in *Ekstra Bladet* in 1948.

From an early time, block makers began to supplement the raised sections of the wooden block with copper nails and strips. The strips and nails allowed for finer detailing and sharpened the lines. When linoleum was invented during the second half of the 19th century, it was embraced as a new material for block printing, in part because it was easier to carve than hardwood. The linoleum was glued onto a wooden block, and the carved image was enhanced with a layer of glued-on felt dust for better absorption of the dye.

Sometimes, so-called repeat nails were added to the edge of the block to produce marks for guiding the alignment of subsequent prints. Still, the finished result often had a certain irregularity, not just in terms of the alignment of the pattern but also in the evenness of colour. For some, these irregularities were just part of the charm of a hand-printed fabric.

Even after screen printing came into widespread use, block printing was not entirely abandoned. In particular, some of generations following Marie Gudme Leth combined screen printing, hand-painting and block printing. Some of the most experimental textile printers of their time used a wide and varied range of printing tools or used conventional printing tools in new and experimental ways.

In the mid-19th century, printers in Lyon, France, refined template printing to develop screen printing, also known as silk screening. At the time, however, screen printing could not compete with the mass production of printed textiles by roller printing machines. Screen printing involves mounting a fine silk mesh on a wooden frame. Today, the frames are made of metal, and the mesh is nylon. To create a negative image, the areas of the silk that are not supposed to transfer ink onto the fabric are lacquered over. The lacquer prevents ink from permeating the silk, so that the fabric maintains its original colour. Ink is applied using a squeegee: a wooden bar with an embedded length of rubber that matched the interior dimensions of the frame. By drawing the squeegee over the distended silk, the printer presses the ink through the mesh and thus transfers the positive image onto the fabric. In multi-colour prints, each colour has its own frame, with different areas of the silk lacquered over. Although screen printing was not an entirely new method, it did enable a technological leap in 20th-century textile printing.

Printing blocks and screens can be used with different types of ink technology and forms of printing. The most common form in Danish textile printing during the 20th century is direct printing. Another printing form, reminiscent of batik, is resist printing, which involves applying substances that prevent dye from permeating the fabric when it is subsequently submerged into a dye bath. In resist printing, the pattern often appears in a negative form on a dyed background. Etching represents a third form, in which the image or pattern is created by etching a dyed fabric to bring out the original colour; in so-called colour etching, a new colour is applied where the original colour was etched away. These are the most elementary forms of printing.

**Helga Foght**
(1902–1974)

**'Harlekin' / 'Harlequin'**
Linen, 1949

During the post-war years, Helga Foght designed a number of patterns inspired by abstract paintings.

The repeat is the smallest recurring element of a continuous pattern. While block printing had a physical limitation to the size of the block, and thus the repeat, a silk screen could be as wide as the full width of the fabric.

Fabrics with small repeats help reduce waste. In curtains, for example, the pattern should line up across the different sections to produce a calm expression. When a fabric has a large repeat, it may be necessary to cut off and discard larger sections to make the pattern line up when the curtains are sewn and hung. This was not very economical, particularly at a time of material shortages.

By the late 1920s, block printing laid the foundation of Danish textile printing. However, the textile printing trade only really gained momentum during the years after the founding of the School of Arts and Crafts in 1930 and the introduction of the school's textile programme in 1931. The first students to graduate from the School of Arts and Crafts established their own workshops. For example, Ruth Hull founded her own studio in 1935, and Helga Foght founded hers in 1937. Many textile printers made the switch from block printing to screen printing during the 1930s.

In 1934, currency restrictions and other regulations hampered the import of crafts and design objects, which gave Danish-made textiles added momentum.

Screen printing became increasingly widespread, and multi-colour prints became easier to make. Student works from the early years of the School of Arts and Crafts show many patterns with small geometric repeats, illustrating that, at this time, the students were taught block printing. The transition from block printing to screen printing took some years to complete, and some later patterns were still based on small units that matched the scale of the printing block or featured motifs that appeared as isolated 'islands', with gaps in between the recurring pattern elements.

Functionalism was not just about a particular design expression: a stringent form combined with the inherent expression of the material, stripped of all superfluous decoration and a focus on simplicity. Style was intertwined with social commitment. The goal was to create liveable homes and simple, utilitarian objects with an industrial design character. This core notion of simple and practical design was a good match for textile printing. The ambition of avoiding ornamentation posed a problem, though, since decorating woven textiles was the very raison d'être of textile printing. That presented a dilemma.

**Marie Gudme Leth**
(1895–1997)

**'Markblomster' / 'Field Flowers'**
Linen, 1940

Marie Gudme Leth's 'Markblomster'
signal the beginning of a new, bold
floral style.

# Marie Gudme Leth

Marie Gudme Leth (1895–1997) in her workshop, which was located in a back building in a courtyard at Rosenvængets Allé 1 in Copenhagen's Østerbro district. The photo shows her working on a version of 'Tripolis med hvid udsparing' (Tripoli with white masked-off areas) that she designed in 1958 as part of her last design, a group of four or five prints.

By the late 1920s, Marie Gudme Leth and Gudrun Stig Aagaard reintroduced textile printing in Denmark. Modernism was gaining ground, leading to a demand for a wider selection of affordable quality textiles. Marie Gudme Leth explicitly aimed to 'elevate textile printing to the same level as other disciplines within Danish decorative arts'.

In 1930, during a stay at the Kunstgewerbeschule (School of Arts and Crafts) in Frankfurt am Main, Marie Gudme Leth was called back to Copenhagen to head the textile printing programme at the newly established School of Arts and Crafts there. The school was located at the Museum of Decorative Art in Bredgade and was the result of the merger of the museum's Craft School, founded in 1901, with the decorative art department at the Technical Society's Schools. The new school taught artistic disciplines, such as drawing, composition and colour studies.

A study tour of a textile factory in Munich in 1934 gave Marie Gudme Leth insight into the screen-printing technology. Compared to block printing, screen printing offered entirely new possibilities. It was not just faster, it was also more accurate. Marie Gudme Leth realized that the screen-printing technology made it possible to produce yard goods in a workshop setting. This in turn brought her closer to her dream of practising textile printing as a decorative art form while creating products that were affordable for a wider audience.

In 1935, Marie Gudme Leth founded the company Dansk Kattuntrykkeri (Danish Calicoe Printing) with support from a number of investors. She had her breakthrough with an exhibition at Magasin-BO in Copenhagen in 1937. That same year, her textiles appeared in the Danish pavilion at the World's Fairs in Paris and, two years later, New York. Marie Gudme Leth made a name for herself with distinctive, elegant leaf and flower prints in a bright and limited colour scale.

Marie Gudme Leth left Dansk Kattuntrykkeri in 1940 and founded an independent studio, which she continued to operate, with a number of assistants, until the 1960s. Looking at her prolific production of printed textiles over this period of about 30 years, we can trace both the technological development from the characteristics of block printing to the possibilities of screen printing and the stylistic development in pattern preferences. She enriched us with beautiful designs, such as 'Meadow Flowers' (1940), 'Guinea Fowl' (1941), 'Cherry' (1946), 'Tripoli' and 'Beirut' (1958).

Marie Gudme Leth was a contemporary of several other talented textile printers, but hers is a particularly rich legacy, both thanks to her innovative – and now classic – patterns and through her teaching at the School of Arts and Crafts. Many regard Marie Gudme Leth as the personification of Danish textile printing, and her status today remains undiminished.

**Marie Gudme Leth**
(1895–1997)

**'Havbund' / 'Seabed'**
Linen, 1936

'Havbund' was designed for and
printed by Dansk Kattuntrykkeri.
The design was in fact screen-printed
but has the characteristics of block
printing, with isolated, well-spaced
elements.

**Marie Gudme Leth**
(1895–1997)

**'Izmir'**
Linen, 1959

The 'Izmir' pattern was one of the last patterns that Marie Gudme Leth created and printed during her approximately 30-year career. Alongside three other patterns, it marked a final culmination to Marie Gudme Leth's body of work.

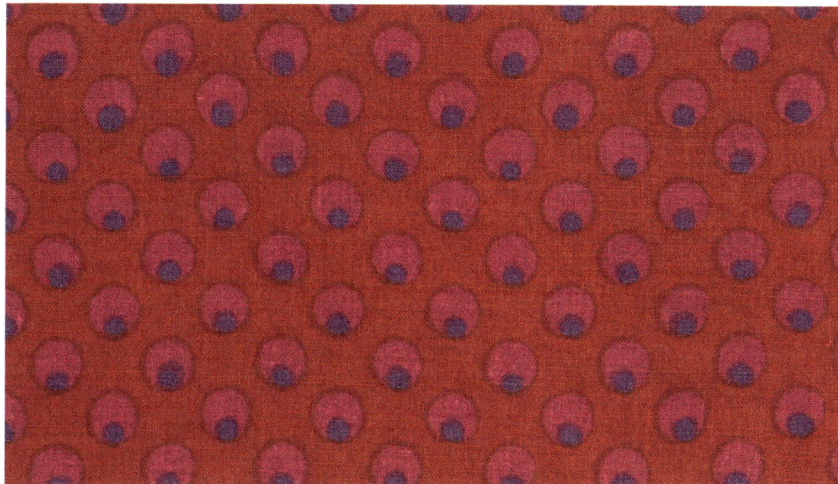

**Marie Gudme Leth**
(1895–1997)

**'Kamæleon' / 'Chameleon'**
English tow fabric, 1938

The individual motifs in the design were also printed on cushion covers.

# Gudrun Stig Aagaard

Gudrun Stig Aagaard was another pioneer of Danish textile printing. Like Marie Gudme Leth, Gudrun Stig Aagaard trained at the School of Drawing and Decorative Art for Women. She continued her studies at Académie des Beaux-Arts des Tissus in Lyon and at I.G. Farbenindustrie in Frankfurt am Main, where she studied the chemistry of dyes and inks. As mentioned above, she experimented with batik, but she began her career as a textile printer by studying and replicating historical printing blocks from museums. She designed new patterns for both block printing and, later, screen printing. Several of her printing blocks are preserved in Designmuseum Danmark's collection.

Compared with the sheer number of designs that were printed in Marie Gudme Leth's studio, Gudrun Stig Aagaard was less prolific. Unfortunately, only a small number of her prints have been preserved at the museum.

Photos of Gudrun Stig Aagaard's printed textiles show her keen understanding of the role of curtains, which need to function in their two characteristic stages – closed and open. Viewers of the Danish TV series *Matador* may have noticed the curtains in Bank Manager Kristen Skjern's swank new bachelor pad. The interior showcased the new and cool design of 1930s functionalism, and of course the curtains were a Gudrun Stig Aagaard design.

Gudrun Stig Aagaard (1895–1986) carving a printing block, probably in linoleum. She established her own studio as early as in 1928, and alongside Marie Gudme Leth, she was one of the pioneers of Danish textile printing. Her first designs were block-printed, but throughout her career, Gudrun Stig Aagaard used both block-printing and screen printing. Unfortunately, only a few of Gudrun Stig Aagaard's textiles have been preserved, even though some of her designs were produced by Cotil.

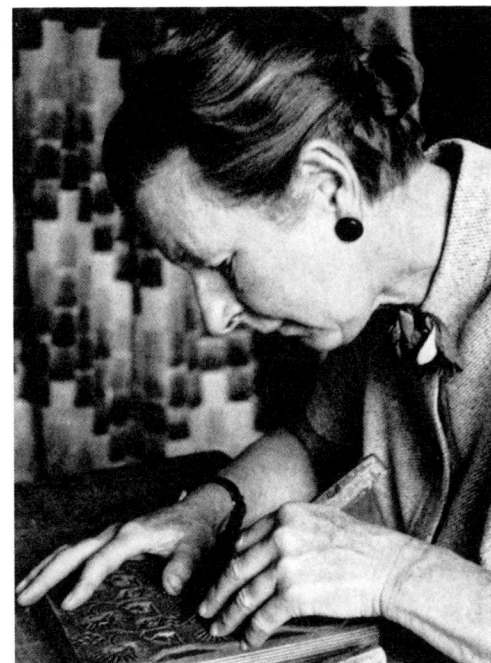

**Gudrun Stig Aagaard**
(1895–1986)

**'Palmette'**
Cotton, 1935–1936

Gudrun Stig Aagaard, who is regarded as one of the pioneers of modern Danish textile printing, probably had a much larger production of both hand-printed and industrial textiles than the museum is able to document.

# Karen Schrader

Some Danish textile prints were created by designers who only had textiles as part of their practice, for example the architect Arne Jacobsen and the ceramic and graphic designer Axel Salto. During the 1930s, two women artists combined textile printing with painting: Karen Schrader and Gudrun Krabbe.

Karen Schrader's artistic practice included drawing, painting, pastels and knitting as well as batik and textile printing. She trained at the Technical School and the Royal Danish Academy of Fine Arts in Copenhagen, followed by a stay at the Kunstgewerbeschule in Munich in 1922. She held her first solo exhibition – pastels and batik – in 1926 in Copenhagen and exhibited jointly with her husband, the painter Kay Christensen, for many years.

Whether Karen Schrader worked with painting or textile printing for furnishing fabrics or clothing, nature and its colour palette were her main source of inspiration. One critic praised her fabrics for clothing, in particular for providing a quality option at a time when good materials were hard to come by because of lingering post-war shortages. As a textile printer, she used both block printing and screen printing.

Several of Karen Schrader's textiles have a similar expression of stylized nature, lushness and light humour as some of Marie Gudme Leth's patterns.

**Karen Schrader**
(1898–1986)

**Fabric section à la rococo**
Linen, 1944

This pattern, designed by Karen Schrader, is a pastiche on French rococo-style silks with imitations of curvy lace ribbons on a background with a small pattern repeat. During the Second World War, several genres of crafts and design revived earlier stylistic periods as a source of comfort during this time of turmoil.

Karen Schrader (1898–1986) made her name as a painter, and for several years, she exhibited alongside her first husband, the painter Kay Christensen (1899–1981). During the initial decades of the textile printing revival in Denmark, the individual printers had very different levels of ambition. Karen Schrader, who remarried after being divorced from her first husband, did not need to earn a living for herself. Perhaps that was why she only sporadically exhibited both visual art and textile prints.

**Karen Schrader**
(1898–1986)

**'Junglen' / 'The Jungle'**
Linen, 1935

Karen Schrader's 'Junglen' pattern follows the narrative style of the time, with the same subtle touch of humour that we recognize in Marie Gudme Leth's contemporary designs.

**Karen Schrader**
(1898–1986)

**'Kavi'**
Cotton, 1945–1960

Many of Karen Schrader's textile prints explored prevailing styles. This print probably dates from the 1940s and follows the same lush, wild flower style as some of Arne Jacobsen's and Marie Gudme Leth's print designs.

**Gudrun Krabbe**
(1900–1976)

**Fish tablecloth**
Linen, 1949

This tablecloth, which was acquired
from a special exhibition held by
Haandarbejdets Fremme in 1949,
was block-printed, Gudrun Krabbe's
preferred method.

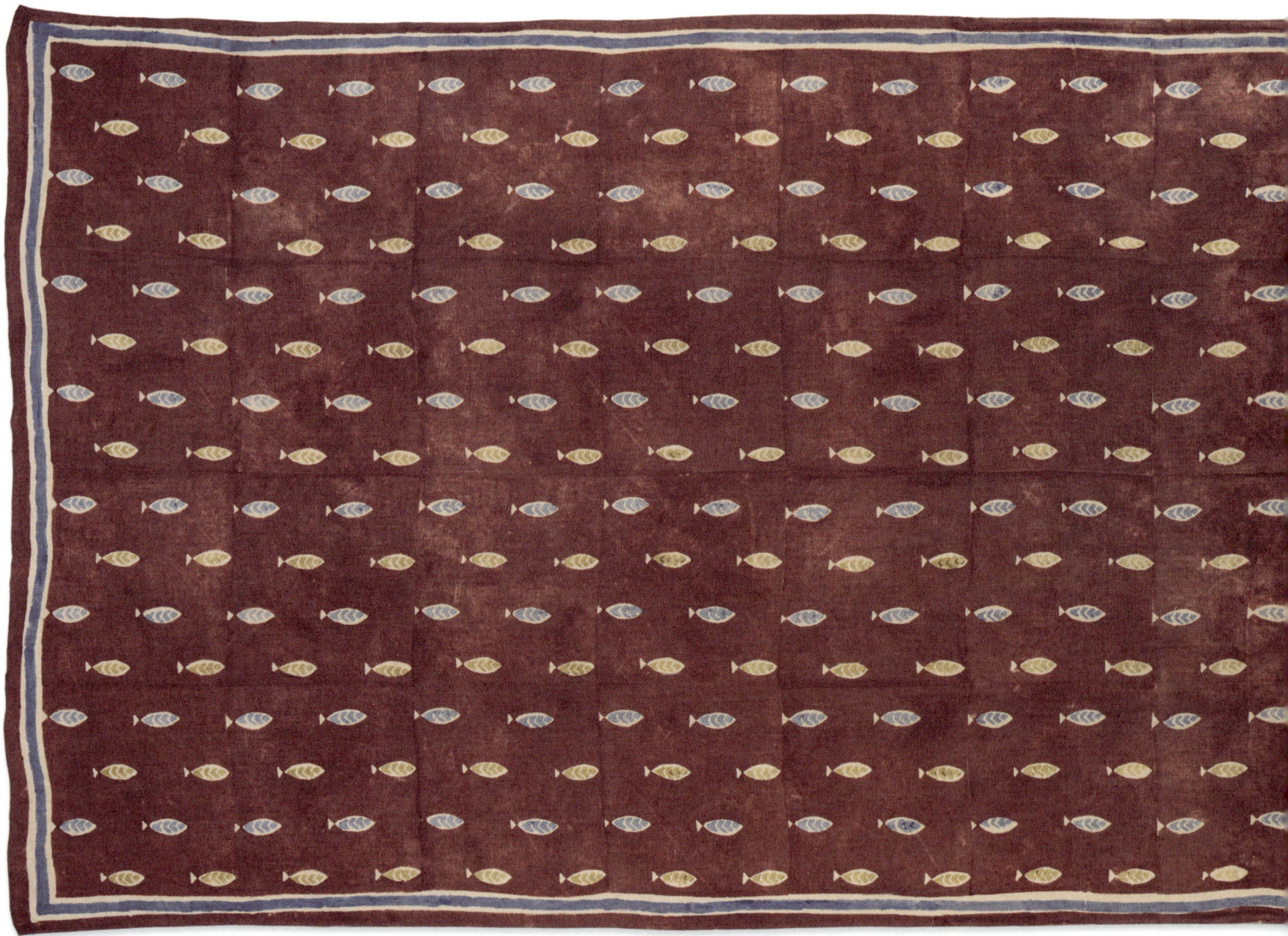

# Gudrun Krabbe

Gudrun Krabbe practised block printing throughout her career. She had trained with the painter Agnes Weie, wife of Edvard Weie. At some point during the 1930s, Gudrun Krabbe learned textile printing from Marie Gudme Leth. It is unclear whether Gudrun Krabbe also learned screen printing. In any case, block printing was her preferred technique. She did textile printing in a workshop she shared with her sister Bodil Bjørn.

A critic wrote that Gudrun Krabbe's prints 'show the marks of the chisel'. Among other terms, he described them as 'stark', suggesting an absence of intricate detailing. Some might call them primitive, while others highlight the 'noble craftsmanship' of her patterns – an expression that reflects its time. Crafts were highly prized during the time around the Second World War. Many places in Europe saw a retro wave in the field of textile printing; a sort of reaction to other developments and a desire to preserve the fundamental values of the discipline. This was manifested in an interest in and appreciation of the hand-crafted expression that block printing represented.

Still, Gudrun Krabbe's craft-oriented printed textiles remained a parenthetical interlude in Danish textile printing. When she died, in 1976, her printing blocks were passed on to an apprentice of hers, Mone Hvass, who continued to print Gudrun Krabbe's patterns well into the 2000s.

In October or November, when daylight became too faint for painting, Gudrun Krabbe (1900–1976) printed textiles. She spent about a month printing, and then the finished fabrics were sewn into tablecloths, table napkins, tea cosies and so forth. In early December, she would hold a sale at her home, where her works sold out in no time. To optimize production, she and her sister, Bodil Bjørn, set up a workshop in a flat on Østerbrogade in Copenhagen. Working with a couple of textile printers, they maintained a production of Gudrun Krabbe's textiles, which were sold from a number of venues, including Den Permanente and Haandarbejdets Fremme shops.

# Modernism

# Modernism

The style of 1940s patterns was characterized by a rich presence of flowers, vines and animals. Many patterns had a decidedly romantic expression. Several designers drew inspiration from historical styles, for example the romantic, cultivated floral patterns of the 18th century. This could be described as a retro wave, a search for reassuring comfort in a tumultuous world through a return to stylistic expressions from the past.

An interior design guide from 1931 recommended choosing light-coloured fabric without a pattern for curtains and hand-woven, monochrome fabrics with a textured pattern for furniture upholstery. In this light, it is interesting to consider the success of Danish textile printing during the late 1930s and into the 1940s and the popularity of many of Marie Gudme Leth's patterns with animals, flowers and bright colours.

Material shortages during and after the Second World War had a big impact on many textile makers and artists, especially weavers. If textile printers were able to get dyestuffs, they could work on ersatz fabrics and textiles from the linen closet, such as sheets and white damask tablecloths, if the household could spare them.

After the dip in Danish textile printing during the Second World War, the craft enjoyed a vibrant post-war revival, as the first generations of graduates from the School of Arts and Crafts established their practices, took part in exhibitions in Denmark and abroad and sold their wares from outlets such as Den Permanente and Illums Bolighus in Copenhagen and the shops of Haandarbejdets Fremme, which were present around the country. In addition to the initial pioneers – Marie Gudme Leth, Gudrun Stig Aagaard and Karen Schrader – practitioners included Ruth Christensen, Helga Foght, Ruth Hull, Inge Ingetoft, Arne Jacobsen, Rolf Middelboe and Dorte Raaschou, among others.

Despite the lingering war-time shortages, the demand for printed textiles was high. After a few years when society and industry had been forced to adapt to difficult conditions, austerity was replaced by boom time, and the market expanded to match the growing demand. The number of trained textile printers making yard goods for furnishing and clothing increased, and with the breakthrough of Danish Design around the world, the export markets too began to show an interest in Danish textile printing. The textile industry made a dedicated effort to market the textiles abroad, assisted by the large travelling exhibitions, including *Design in Scandinavia: An exhibition of objects for the home*, which was on the road from 1954 to 1957, and *The Arts of Denmark* from 1960 to 1961.

The patterns gradually moved away from the naturalist and romantic retro wave in favour of abstract or geometric textiles with small repeats in bright, crisp colours. While many patterns were previously printed in linen or synthetic fabrics, for example *vistra*, a heavy cotton quality now became the norm. Several classic patterns were created during this period. Some saw the 1950s as the decade of 'frank' designs – it was certainly a decade of pronounced optimism. Perhaps that was why collaborations between textile designers and industry were so successful during the 1950s. There was a strong preference for tasteful, versatile and high-quality textiles.

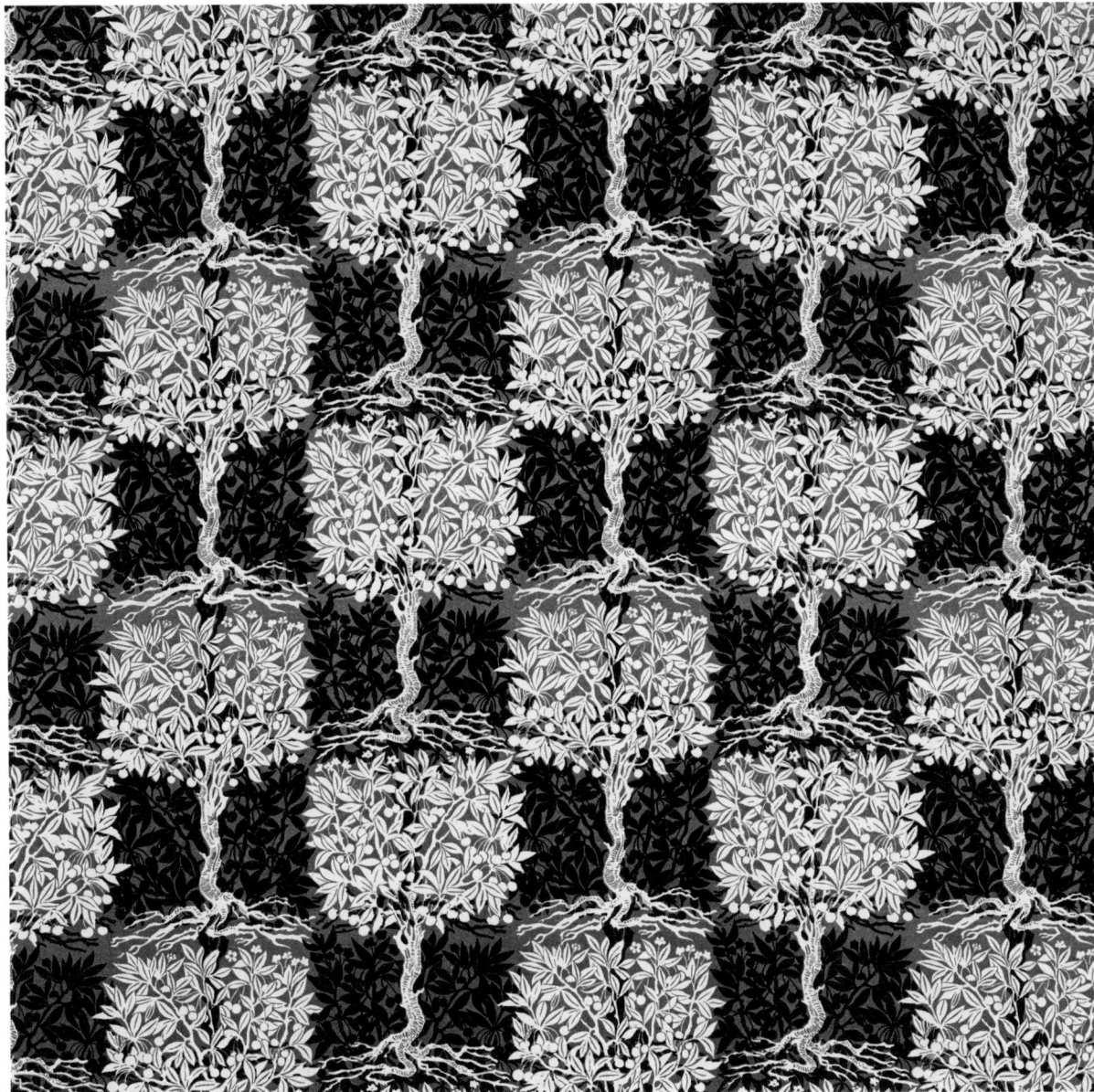

**Bent Karlby**
(1912–1998)

**'The Orchard'**
Cotton, 1945–1960

Bent Karlby was a Danish architect
and designer, who is best known for
his lighting and wallpaper designs,
including for the wallpaper factories
C. Krügers Tapetfabrik and Brdr. Dahls
Tapetfabrik. Manufacturer unknown.

Several artists designed textiles to be sold by the yard. Since many textile printers were inspired by modern, abstract art, it seemed a logical move for the textile manufacturers to engage artists to design textile print designs.

During the 1960s, the Danish textile industry was working at a rapid pace. While factories had previously bought pattern designs abroad, they now often worked with Danish designers. At the same time, competition from abroad was intensifying. Towards the end of the decade, the market began to react – the competition became too heated, and Danish companies struggled to compete on price. Abroad, pattern designs became increasingly bold and playful. The inspiration came from American pop art and British pop music, but these trends were not immediately obvious in Danish textile printing.

**Børge Glahn**
(1917–1991)

**'Soulage'**
Cotton, 1955–1965

As a young architect typical of his time, Børge Glahn believed in growth and progress. He designed projects that would seem fairly radical today. He designed patterns for L.F. Foght, but no manufacturer is recorded for 'Soulage'.

The time from 1940 and into the 1960s was a golden age for Danish textile printing. Danish makers and artists had a strong showing in numerous exhibitions both in Denmark and abroad. The patterns showed a greater freedom of expression, and many textile printers experimented with imaginative and unusual printing methods. Some textile printers pursued artistic expressions in bespoke compositions, without a repeat, designed for decorative textile projects in private homes and public space.

Retrospective reviews of Danish design, both in Denmark and abroad, have not assigned a key role to textile printing. At the time, however, textile printing did enjoy a prominent position. Danish textile printers participated in exhibitions on equal footing with other design disciplines. Printed textiles were available from all the leading decorative art and design shops, and Danish journals and magazines gave the textile printers equal coverage to other craftspeople and designers.

However, in a review in a 1955 issue of the magazine published by Haandarbejdets Fremme, museum curator Hans Lassen of the National Museum of Denmark wrote that 'Printed textiles are utilitarian items used for curtains, drapes, bedspreads, runners, upholstery fabrics, tablecloths, napkins etc., etc., meaning that they are an accompaniment. But they are an accompaniment that is deeply important for the interior. The wrong choice results in disjointed, unsettled rooms – dreadful to be in. Conversely: chosen in accordance with the character and usage, they lend a sense of restful calm to the rooms. This is true both at home and out, in private rooms and public settings.' It would take about 25 years before printed fabrics were no longer seen as a mere accompaniment.

**Nina Koppel**
(1942–1990)

**Length of fabric for dress pyjamas**
Silk, 1966

Nina Koppel graduated from the School of Arts and Crafts in Copenhagen in 1966 and established her own firm that same year. She worked with several different manufacturers and created upholstery fabrics and rugs for Halling-Koch Design Center, Kvadrat, Kevi, Magasin du Nord and Textil-Lassen. She also created clothing, including in collaboration with the designer Jean Voigt from 1966 to 1967.

**Ruth Christensen**
(1918–2007)

**Wall hanging**
Silk, 1960–1970

Throughout her career, Ruth Christensen's work included printing and painting free compositions without a repeat for decorative purposes.

# Ruth Christensen

Because of the impact of the Second World War, Ruth Christensen was delayed in beginning her training as an artist. After the end of the war, she went to Paris. Here, in addition to learning French, she spent time with resident Danish artists, including the painter Mogens Andersen and the painter, sculptor and designer Gunnar Aagaard Andersen, whom she met through her older brother, graphic artist Povl Christensen. In 1950, she graduated from the textile printing line of the School of Arts and Crafts.

Ruth Christensen designed a few patterns that were put into industrial production. She was more interested in printing and painting one-off decorative pieces with a repeat, using printing blocks and small screens as flexible elements. Block printing as direct printing, resistant printing and/or etching combined with painting or dabbing ink onto the fabric with a sponge gave her the freedom to create decorative textile hangings as well as fabrics for clothing. The combination of different techniques and the use of intense, saturated colours give her textiles a vibrant, shimmering, three-dimensional expression.

Thematically, her wall hangings fall into two categories: abstract and narrative. In her narrative textile hangings, the images are usually flowering gardens with fantastical animals, trees and plants. In several of her textiles, she experimented with the addition of machine embroidery beading and sewn-on mirrors. These exuberant narrative textile hangings found a receptive audience abroad.

In addition to her training at the School of Arts and Crafts, Ruth Christensen (1918–2007) spent a year working at Marie Gudme Leth's studio. She created printed textiles for clothing, among other uses. In 1970, she was asked to print fabric for a long evening gown that Queen Ingrid wore at an event during a state visit to Ethiopia, hosted by Emperor Haile Selassie. The Queen had bought white silk in Rome, which Ruth Christensen decorated with prints of Danish field flowers and gold pigment. The dress, which had a modest design with long sleeves and no decolletage, was created by fashion designer Jørgen Bender (1938–1999).

During the 1950s and 1960s, she worked with fabrics for clothing that were used to create trendy fashion and displayed in solo exhibitions, including in a critically acclaimed exhibition in 1958 in the Haandarbejdets Fremme shop at Kongens Nytorv in central Copenhagen. At this exhibition, the Museum of Decorative Art acquired the first of her pieces for its collection. She presented her artisanal clothing designs in countless exhibition and runway shows along with several other contemporary textile artists.

Even at a ripe old age, Ruth Christensen never lost her urge to experiment with her art, and she continued to work with textiles in other ways than the physically demanding practice of textile printing. She designed embroidery patterns for Haandarbejdets Fremme, for example a series of bags with a combination of cross stich and petit point.

Unlike other decorative art genres, little has been published about textile printing in Danish. In 1975, Ruth Christensen's insightful book *Tekstiltryk – historie, farver og teknik* (Textile Printing: History, colours and technique) was released by the publishing house Gyldendal. As suggested by the title, the book ranged from historical information to descriptions of printing techniques.

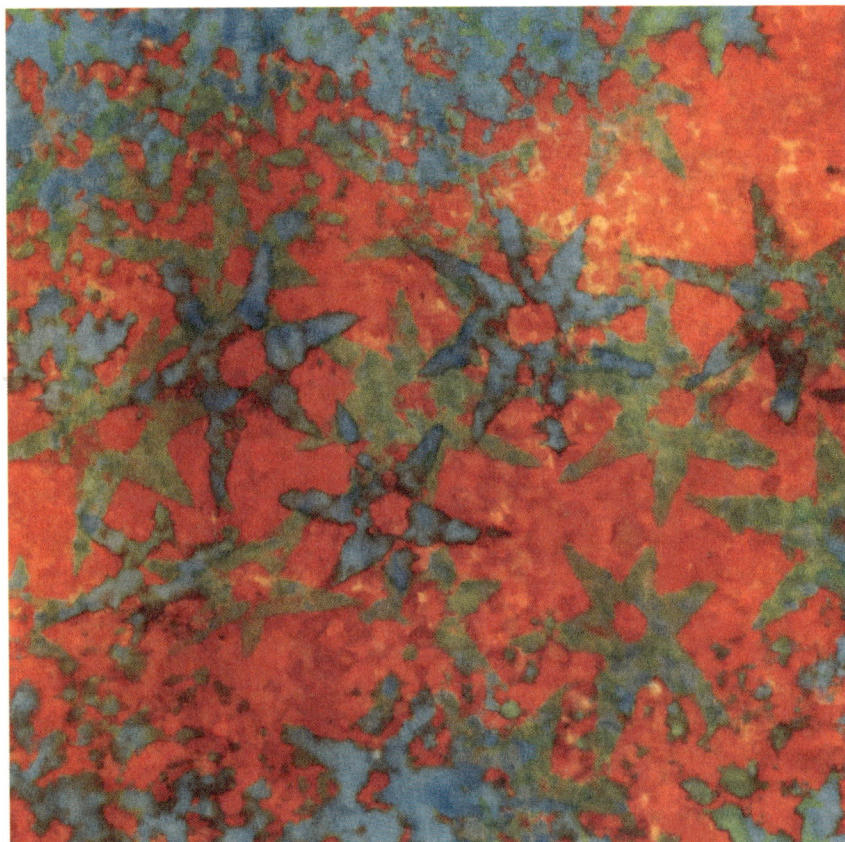

**Ruth Christensen**
(1918–2007),
pattern design and printing

**Birthe Gorell**
(b.1931),
dress design and sewing

**Silk dress**
1958

The museum bought this silk dress
from Ruth Christensen's exhibition
at Haandarbejdets Fremme in 1958.
It was the first contemporary dress
purchased by the museum.

# Helga Foght

Helga Foght graduated from the School of Arts and Crafts in 1937, at the age of 35. Concurrent with her studies there, she completed a two-year embroidery course at the school operated by Haandarbejdets Fremme. Originally, she wanted to be an embroidery designer, as she had taken an interest in folk embroidery through her work as a secretary at Askov Folk High School.

Along with the textile printer Ruth Hull, Helga Foght was among the first of Marie Gudme Leth's students to later build a career in the field. At the School of Arts of Crafts, she learned block printing, but when she established her first studio in 1938, in the Copenhagen district of Christianshavn, she began to work with screen printing. In 1949, she employed Inge Ingetoft as a studio assistant. They continued to work together until Helga Foght's death, in 1974. In the meantime, they had moved into a house in Gentofte as their shared home and studio. In 1969, they formalized their partnership by establishing the joint company I/S Foght og Ingetoft.

Fairly soon after her graduation, Helga Foght established connections to several architects and landed large-scale interior design commissions. In 1939, she initiated a partnership about printed furnishing fabrics with the textile wholesale company L.F. Fogh. As a result, her patterns were printed in larger production runs, which kept down the price of the fabrics and made them affordable to a wider audience. She was given free hands to work with patterns, colours and materials and had much greater freedom to experiment than she would normally have had in a collaboration with industry. In addition to developing her own patterns for industrial production, she printed smaller series of designs by other artists, including by Axel Salto.

Helga Foght's patterns from the 1930s and 1940s were stylized nature-inspired patterns. Her breakthrough happened during the years after the Second World War, when her patterns came to focus more on the interaction of colours, lines, rhythms and movement. Helga Foght's new designs were inspired by abstract art, and the patterns have an unusual and bold but also simple and confident expression, as exemplified by 'Fuga', 'Pavane', 'Harlekin' (Harlequin) and 'Abstraktion' (Abstraction).

Helga Foght was very active in her field, exhibiting widely, serving as on several boards and teaching at the School of Arts and Crafts, from 1954 to 1970, and in other textile education contexts.

Helga Foght sometimes suffered the indignity of having her prints from the 1940s regarded as derivative of Marie Gudme Leth's work. In hindsight, this seems quite unfair. Textile patterns were influenced by contemporary fashions and general trends in culture, art and society. Most textile printers simply followed the style of the times – including Helga Foght.

Helga Foght (1902–1974) was one of the most prolific textile printers from the mid-1930s to about 1970 as a contemporary of Marie Gudme Leth, who was her teacher at the School of Arts and Crafts. In addition to the large design exhibitions that toured North America, she exhibited in Norway and Sweden. She also exhibited at the Milan Triennial in 1951, where she received a gold medal.

**Helga Foght**
(1902–1974)

**'Orientalsk' / 'Oriental'**
Vistra, 1937

The motif in Helga Foght's print from 1937 has Oriental inspiration but also brings to mind the Swiss psychiatrist Hermann Rorschach's (1884–1922) famous inkblot test.

**Helga Foght**
(1902–1974)

**'Fuga' / 'Fugue'**
Cotton, 1951

The patterns that Helga Foght designed during the late 1940s were quite extraordinary in their interplay of movement, rhythm, colours and lines.

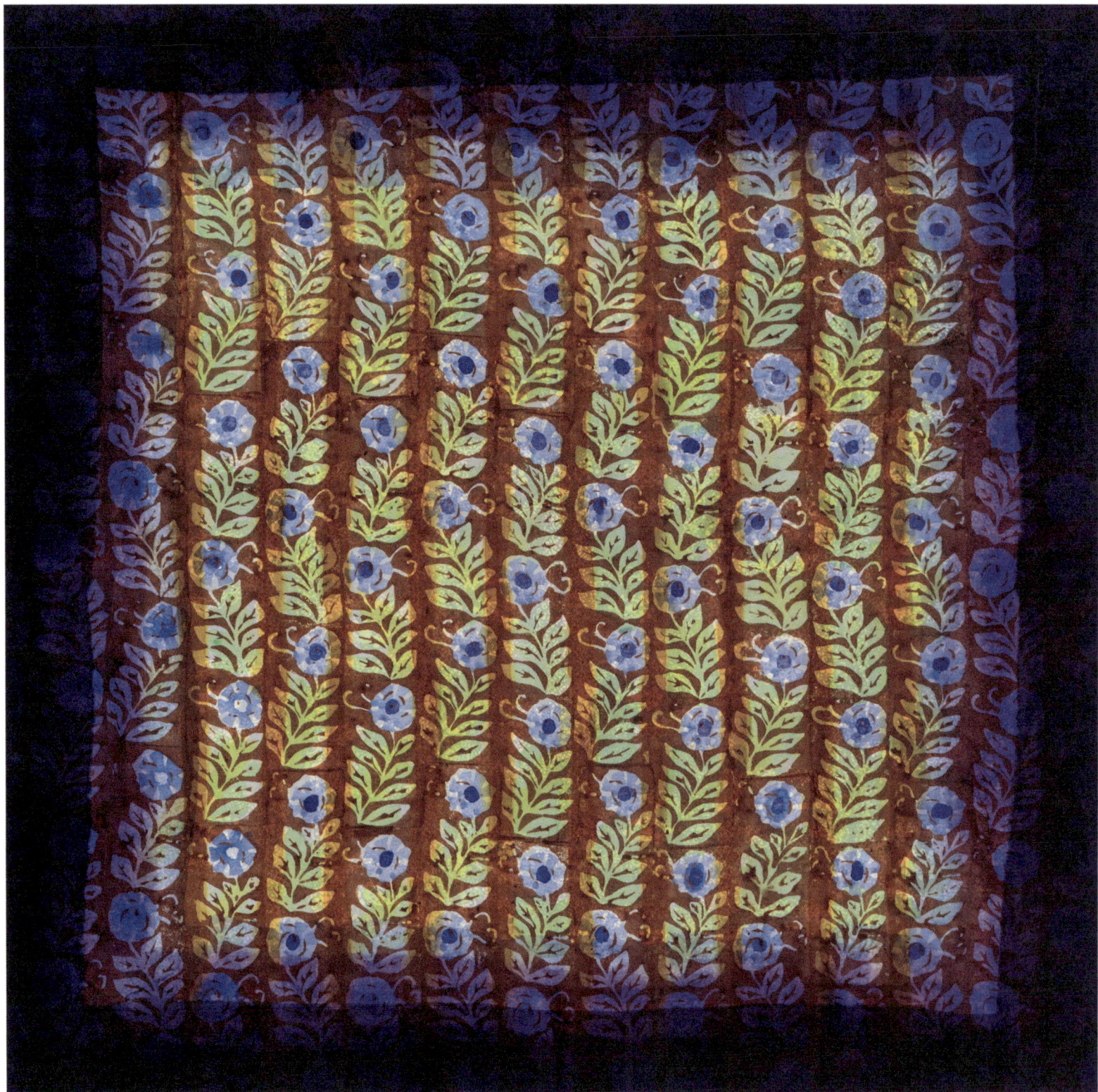

# Ruth Hull

Ruth Hull belonged to the first generation of textile print graduates from the School of Arts and Crafts in Copenhagen who had been taught by Marie Gudme Leth. She graduated in 1935, founded her own studio that same year and took part in Kunstnernes Efterårsudstilling (the Artists' Autumn Exhibition) in 1936. Like Gudrun Stig Aagaard, Ruth Hull copied historical printing blocks from the 18th and 19th centuries. She also practised screen printing but never quite gave up block printing. Whether her early prints were created using screen or block printing, they all featured recurring motifs with a uniform colour scheme.

Ruth Hull is remembered for her diverse and varied artistic expression and technical experiments, including block printing, painting directly on the textile, tie-dyeing and resistant printing. Her colours ranged from delicate shades to high-intensity hues, with gradation or high contrast. She was one of the most experimental textile printers of her time. For example, she broadened the concept of the colour block to include wine corks or flannel-wrapped rods.

Painting directly on the textile liberated the textile printer from the structure of repeats. Even though some of her patterns were industrially produced by Unika-Væv and Cotil, most of her later production consisted of fabrics in complete holistic compositions and one-off fabrics for dresses that were sold by Haandarbejdets Fremme.

In her youth, Ruth Hull (1912–1996) designed small-repeat patterns for the Swedish textile industry. Later, after establishing her own studio, she excelled at utilizing the simple techniques of textile printing that were possible in a one-person workshop. At one point, for example, she began to paint directly on the textiles, a technique that did not require the same degree of precision as block- or screen-printing pattern repeats. Her textiles had a free, artistic and painterly approach, which was also evident in the printed textiles created by her apprentice Bodil Bødtker-Næss.

**Ruth Hull**
(1912–1996)

**Scarf**
Silk, 1950–1960

In this scarf, Ruth Hull experimented with colour gradation.

**Ruth Hull**
(1912–1996)

**Length of fabric**
Cotton, 1950–1960

In this print, Ruth Hull appears to have practised tie-dyeing. Several colours have been painted on the textile, the darker colour possibly by means of an instrument, perhaps a tjanting, which is traditionally used for batik.

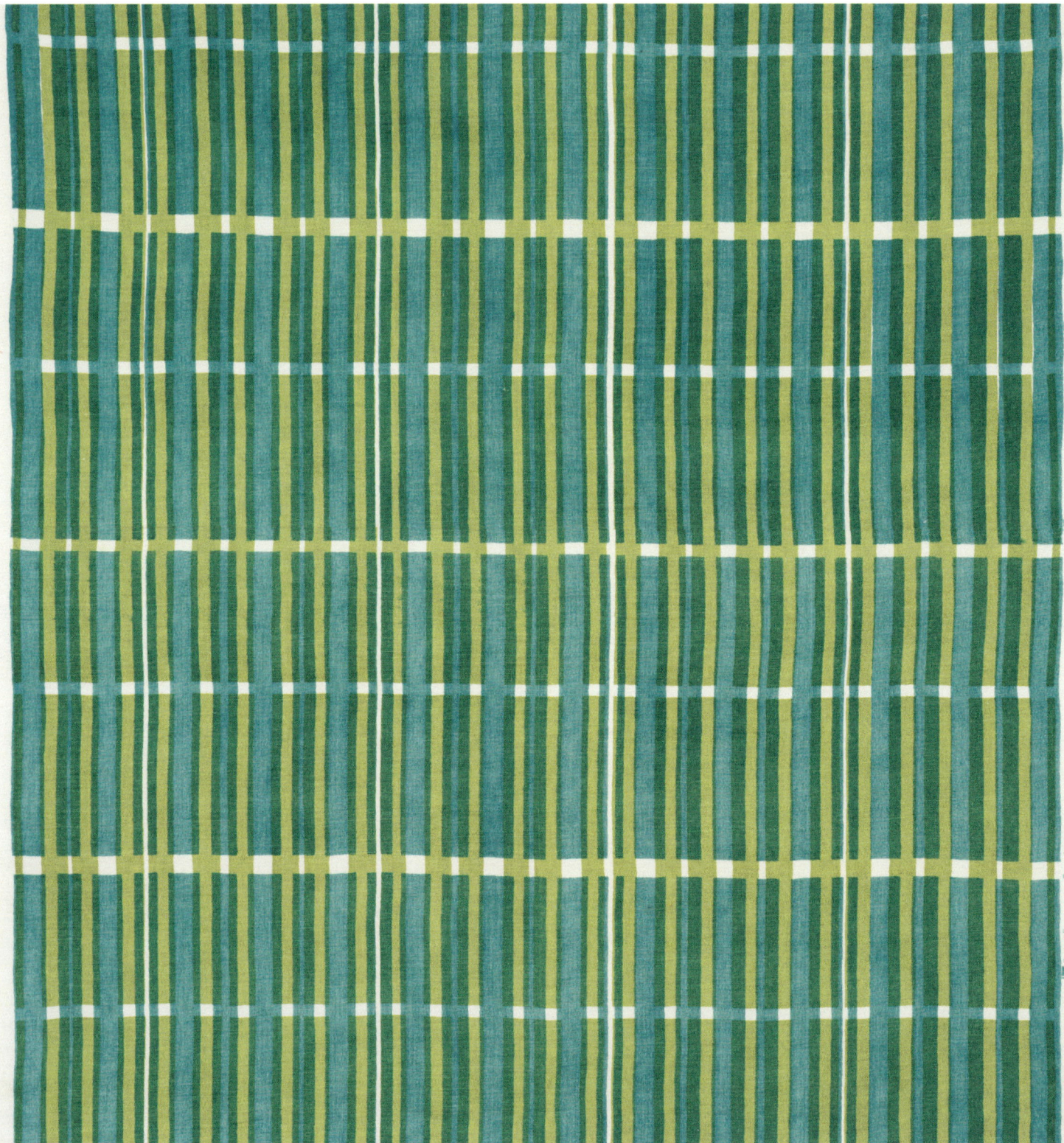

# Inge Ingetoft

Inge Ingetoft – or simply Ingetoft, as she was mostly known – apprenticed in Helga Foght's studio. In 1954, the two founded a joint studio with Ingetoft at the helm. Like Helga Foght, Ingetoft was a prolific textile printer, designing a large number of patterns that were produced for the L.F. Foght brand.

Most of Ingetoft's printed designs had a striking simplicity. She mastered the art of designing textiles that could serve as a calm background for the other furnishings in home interiors without becoming bland or anonymous. Like Gudrun Stig Aagaard, she designed curtain fabric motifs with consideration for the appearance and folds of the fabric when in use.

Ingetoft was inspired by modernist architecture, and her ornamentation was minimal but elegant. The abstract patterns had a confident expression and regular rhythm with a good distribution of decoration and a simplified use of colour in each print. Her most convincing patterns had a monochrome printed surface interrupted by abstract line drawings in the white original tone of the fabric, such as her 1950s patterns 'Kontiki', 'Ceylon', 'Congo' and 'Cambodia', all of which were printed by L.F. Foght. In her abstract pattern 'Profiler' (Profiles), the whitish colour of the fabric is included as an added 'colour' in the pattern. Thus, the original colour of the fabric is not perceived as the background that other shapes and colours are printed on but as an equal component. Inge Ingetoft fully mastered the process of adapting her designs to the conditions of modern mass production.

Inge Ingetoft (1929–1996) and her partner, Helga Foght, were among the women textile printers who established a company with a well-functioning workshop where they could earn a decent living for themselves and their staff. During the 1970s and 1980s, however, the economics became increasingly difficult. After Helga Foght's death, in 1974, Inge Ingetoft took on commissions for commercial companies and also printed a few antependia, including for the Church of the Holy Spirit and the Citadel Chapel in Copenhagen.

**Inge Ingetoft**
(1929–1996)

**'Korea'**
Cotton, 1955

Inge Ingetoft's textiles were well suited for home interiors, as the calm pattern surfaces provided a coherent and unifying expression for the many diverse elements in the home.

**Inge Ingetoft**
(1929–1996)

**'Profiler' / 'Profiles'**
Cotton, 1953

'Profiler' was printed
in duotone, but the
background colour of the
fabric features as a shape
of equal significance as
the blue and brownish
green shapes.

**Inge Ingetoft**
(1929–1996)

**'Indus'**
Cotton, 1970

As underscored by the title, Inge
Ingetoft's pattern was influenced by
the many imported ethnic fabrics that
were fashionable in both clothing and
interior design around 1970.

**Arne Jacobsen**
(1902–1971)

**'Rågekoloni' / 'Crows Nest' [sic]**
for Textil-Lassen
Cotton, 1951

The architect Arne Jacobsen designed textile print patterns in collaboration with several textile manufacturers, including Textil-Lassen.

# Arne Jacobsen

As a young man, the architect Arne Jacobsen (1902–1971) dreamt of becoming a painter. Instead, he became a architect. In his later life, he dreamt of being a gardener. He merged his two dreams in watercolour paintings of nature. Together with his wife, the trained textile printer Jonna Jacobsen, he fled to Sweden during the Second World War. Unable to work as an architect, he turned instead to watercolours. By many accounts, he received his wife's help with translating these nature studies into repetitive textile patterns.

From 1943 and into the 1960s, the architect Arne Jacobsen created a large number of printed textile designs. He began this production in 1943, during his war-time exile in Sweden. That same year, he married Jonna Jacobsen (née Møller), who had trained as a textile printer under Marie Gudme Leth. Jonna Jacobsen helped develop Arne Jacobsen's drawings and watercolours into textile patterns. While in Sweden, he established a collaboration with Nordiska Kompaniet (NK), a Swedish department store founded in 1902. The textiles were created for NK's Textilkammare, which was headed by the Swedish textile artist Astrid Sampe from 1937 to 1971. NK worked with some of the leading Nordic textile designers. As early as 1944, the department store held a large exhibition presenting 16 of Arne Jacobsen's printed patterns and framed design studies. This exhibition marked Arne Jacobsen's breakthrough as a textile designer, and the Swedish Nationalmuseum bought 12 patterns for their collection. Back in Denmark after the war, Arne Jacobsen continued to design and paint patterns for printed textiles, which were produced by several Danish textile manufacturers, including Grautex, Textil-Lassen and, not least, C. Olesen's brand Cotil.

The same stylistic influences that characterize the patterns of most textile printers are also seen in Arne Jacobsen's textiles. Marie Gudme Leth's botanical patterns were inspired by garden flowers, often arranged into bouquets and slightly stylized. Arne Jacobsen's plant motifs, on the other hand, were lush, wild nature with naturalist flowers and plants, sometimes entire plant environments. After his return from Sweden, the inspirations from wild nature were gradually replaced by patterns in which the repeat itself stood out more. His patterns for Cotil from the 1950s and 1960s had a supple, geometric and graphic expression.

**Arne Jacobsen**
(1902–1971)

**'Foldblad' / 'White Hellebore'**
for Textil-Lassen
Cotton, 1960–1970

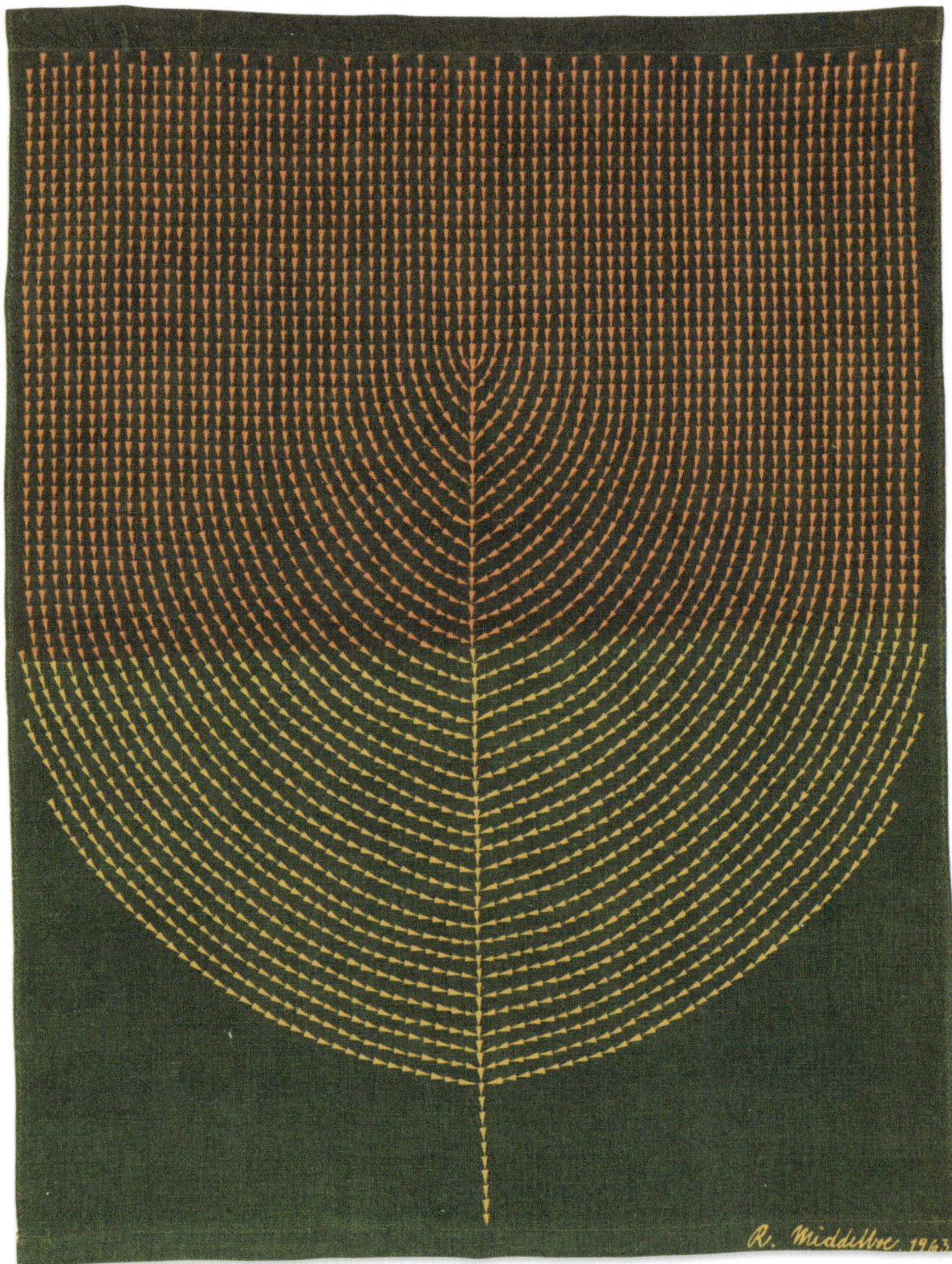

**Rolf Middelboe**
(1917–1995)

**Small wall hanging**
Linen, 1963

Some of Rolf Middelboe's later prints
had a graphic expression.

# Rolf Middelboe

Rolf Middelboe trained as a graphic designer at the School of Arts and Crafts in Copenhagen from 1934 to 1937 and as a textile printer from 1939 to 1940. He established his own textile printing studio in 1941, and in 1944, he became the artistic director of Dansk Kattuntryk (Danish Calico Print), previously Dansk Kattuntrykkeri. Several of his patterns were printed at Dansk Kattuntryk, which also produced textiles by other designers. From 1953, he also worked with the weaving mill Unika-Væv. His earliest patterns were stylized representations of nature, as was the case for other textile printers. During the early 1950s, he moved towards images and patterns inspired by abstract art and geometric shapes. Over the years, he developed a more graphic and precise expression that was adapted to the functional purpose or intended form. For example, he designed patterns for tablecloths to match the shape of a round table.

Rolf Middelboe not only worked as a textile printer but also as a graphic and colour designer, including as a colour consultant for the Danish national railway service DSB from 1972 to 1978 and for the wallpaper factory Dahls Tapetfabrik. Rolf Middelboe taught textile printing at the School of Arts and Crafts in Copenhagen from 1957 to 1964, functioned as an external examiner at the School of Arts and Crafts in Kolding and served as president of IDD, Industrial Designers Denmark.

Many of Rolf Middelboe's (1917–1995) female colleagues saw his textile expression as a break with common practice. Perhaps this was because Rolf Middelboe did not limit his design work to textiles. His textiles were produced in partnership with the manufacturer Halling-Koch, who founded Unika Væv and later the Halling-Koch Design Center and also designed a few pieces of furniture. In 1975, Rolf Middelboe designed the colour scheme for the new Ikea building in Tåstrup; his colour design was altered in a renovation in 2010.

**Rolf Middelboe**
(1917–1995)

**Tablecloth**
Cotton, 1960–1970

Rolf Middelboe not only worked
as a textile printer but also as
a graphic designer.

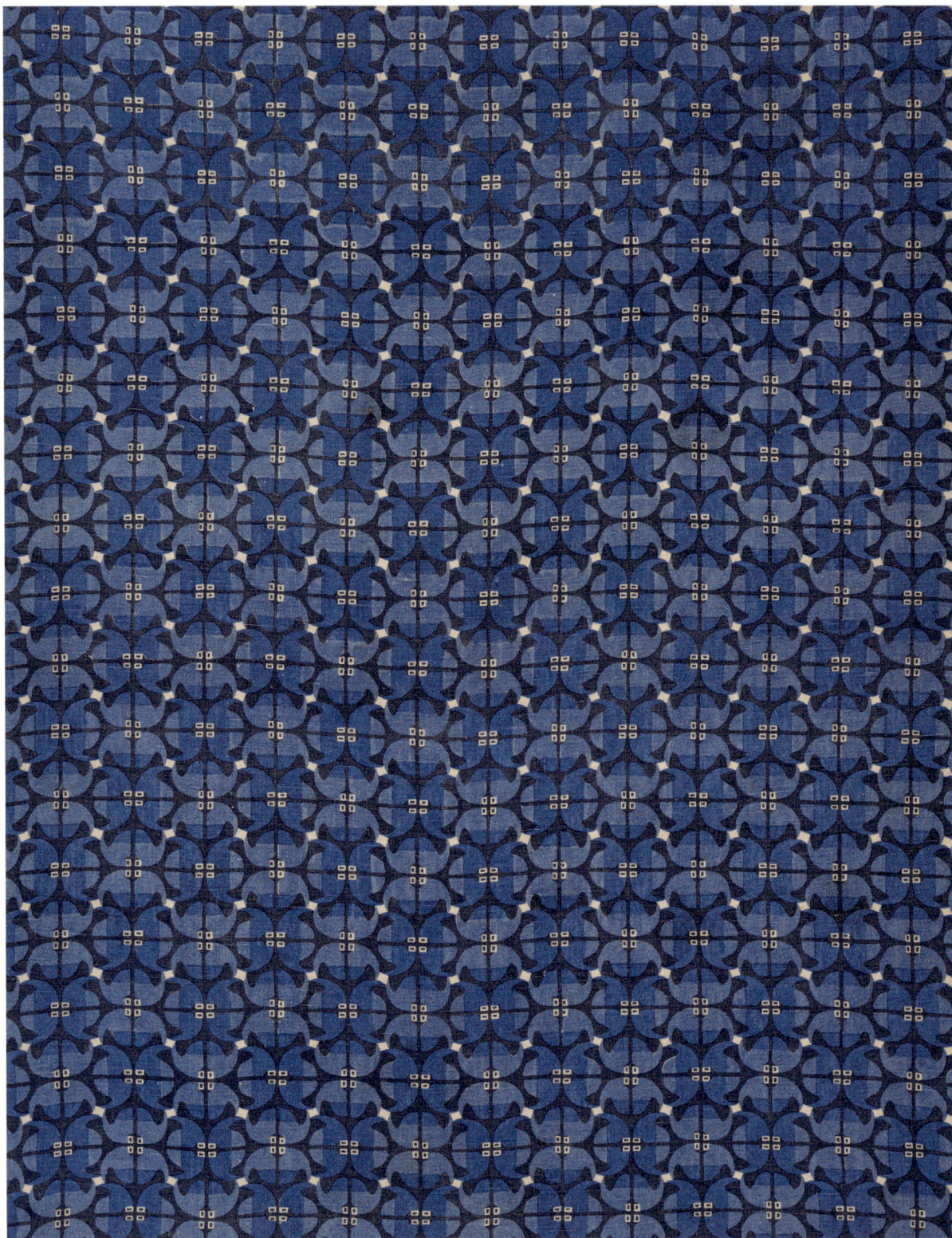

**Dorte Raaschou**
(1929–2011)

**'Krebsens Vendekreds'**
**/ 'Tropic of Cancer'**
for Cotil
Linen, 1957–1965

Over a period of eight years, Dorte
Raaschou created a large number of
designs for Cotil, including 'Krebsens
Vendekreds'.

# Dorte Raaschou

Looking back at her time at the School of Arts and Crafts, Dorte Raaschou (1929–2011) considered it very inadequate – a view shared by several other students from the same period. This was after Marie Gudme Leth had stopped teaching there, and many of the classes were taught by short-term temps. One fixed point for many of the students was the weaver Franka Rasmussen (1907–1994), who taught the students to 'respect the gap': encouraging the students to incorporate the gap in between the motifs as a regular pattern element. The photo shows Dorte Raaschou at her dining table, which also served as her printing table. The printing blocks on the wall are purely decorative.

As a textile printer, Dorte Raaschou left a strong legacy, both in the form of her beautiful and poetic hand-printed and industrially produced textiles and as a teacher at the School of Arts and Crafts in Copenhagen. Dorte Raaschou's interest in textiles was sparked by a visit to the large exhibitions that Haandarbejdets Fremme held at the Museum of Decorative Art every three years. Through family members, Dorte Raaschou got in touch with the textile printer Ruth Hull, who encouraged her to apply to the School of Arts and Crafts in Copenhagen. Among her teachers was the textile printer Ingermarie Ostenfeld, who taught block printing. After the war, textile printers embraced a wider span of techniques, and block printing enjoyed a minor renaissance. Several decorative artists combined screen printing with block printing and other techniques. Dorte Raaschou graduated from the school in 1951.

Like many other textile printers at the time, Dorte Raaschou established a studio in her parents' home. It was difficult for an unmarried woman to rent a flat. The difficulty of establishing an independent studio and the primitive conditions that many decorative artists had to work under makes their achievements all the more impressive. Dorte Raaschou printed textiles in her room and rinsed out the excess dye in her parents' bathroom. When the parents moved to a larger flat, she set up a printing table in a separate room. Dorte Raaschou practised block printing, since her cramped workspace did not allow for the larger printing screens. She spent a year working in Marie Gudme Leth's studio, where she learned a great deal more about dyes, inks and printing methods and about being structured and systematic in her work. She was very inspired by Marie Gudme Leth's late geometric textile designs, where the entire surface was filled out, and the interplay of colour was the main focus.

In 1956, she found a fifth-floor flat of just 52 m2 in Puggaardsgade in Copenhagen. Conditions there were still primitive, but she still managed to print a large number of textiles. She practised both block and screen printing but preferred the block. To fix the ink to the fabric, she steamed the printed textile in a steamer over a gas cooker in her kitchen before rinsing it in a bathtub that she had installed in her kitchen. Fabric was expensive, so she bought short lengths of unprinted silk from the fabric shop Per Reumert on Strøget in central Copenhagen. Half of her working table was dedicated to printing pre-measured lengths of silk or wool. A seamstress occupied the other half, sewing dresses, blouses and skirts that were sold from the Copenhagen design shop Den Permanente.

In 1957, Dorte Raaschou struck up a partnership with C. Olesen's brand Cotil, which took over the task of printing her cotton and linen yard goods. Her designs for Cotil included 'Digitalis', 'Gøgeurt' (Marsh Orchid), 'Krebsens Vendekreds' (Tropic of Cancer), 'Nuoro', 'Prismer' (Prisms), 'Stenbuk' (Capricorn), 'Strega' and 'Sværmerier' (Reveries) (1957–1964), all printed in several colour variants. She worked for Cotil for eight years and was the first recipient of the Cotil Prize in 1962.

Like so many other textile printers, Dorte Raaschou struggled to make a living from her trade, so to supplement her income, she taught at the School of Arts and Crafts in Copenhagen from 1964 to 1981. By then, the school had been renamed the School of Decorative Art.

**Dress coupon**
Silk, 1950–1960

Dorte Raaschou printed
silk coupons (lengths of silk
measured out for a particular
item of clothing), mainly as
block printing, at the dining table
in her home.

**Dorte Raaschou**
(1929–2011)

**'Digitalis'**
for Cotil
Cotton, 1957–1965

Dorte Raaschou's 'Digitalis' was
produced in several colourways.

**Axel Salto**
(1889–1961)

**'Keramik' / 'Ceramics'**
Cotton, 1949

In his 'Keramik' print, Axel Salto
creates a three-dimensional pattern
on the two-dimensional surface by
manipulating the viewer's perception
of foreground and background.

# Axel Salto

In April 1945, the painter, graphic artist and ceramic artist Axel Salto presented the first printed patterns to be produced for L.F. Foght. The works had been underway for about a year, and the crop included 'Aks' (Ear of corn), 'Glæden' (Joy), 'Persisk' (Persian) and 'Mandarin'. Most of the prints were carried out by Helga Foght, one by Brita Drewsen and Gudrun Clemens's company, Den Blaa Fabrik (The Blue Factory). Axel Salto had previously worked with patterns for book binding, and some of these patterns now served as the point of departure for his textile work.

The source of inspiration for Axel Salto's patterns – and his art overall – was a fascination with nature and its shapes and structures. In some of his patterns, the nature inspiration was fairly concrete; in others, it was more stylized and abstract but still recognizable. The patterns included stylized leaves, ears of corn, sprouting onions – pointing to his so-called sprouting style – tulips, fruits and other forms of nature. His designs applied different scales. Patterns with small repeats were well suited for curtains, while the larger repeats required larger surfaces to appear to their full advantage. Axel Salto worked with patterns for textile printing for about ten years.

Axel Salto's 'Keramik' (Ceramic) pattern features nine of his own ceramic pieces in a design that plays with our perception of background and foreground. A topic and an effect that he returned to in 'Vaserne' (the Vases) from 1952. His more complex motifs 'Persisk', 'Grotesque', both from 1945, and 'Antilope' (Antelope), from 1949, feature deer, one of Salto's favourite graphic images.

Axel Salto (1889–1961) at the Museum of Decorative Art (now Designmuseum Danmark) in 1954, where he held a solo exhibition. To the left of the large ceramic vessel, there is a woodcut (or lithograph) showing the motif that he used for his textile print 'Gro' (Grow), which is shown on page 98. Several of the decorative motifs and patterns that he used for book covers – his so-called Salto Papers – were reused on other scales in many of his textiles.

**Axel Salto**
(1889–1961)

**'Persisk' / 'Persian'**
Linen, 1945

**Axel Salto**
(1889–1961)

**'Gro' / 'Grow'**
Cotton, 1954

The sprouting onion in the 'Gro'
pattern positions the design
as part of Axel Salto's so-called
sprouting style.

# Grete Ehs Østergaard

Grete Ehs Østergaard enrolled at the School of Arts and Crafts in Copenhagen in 1954, just 16 years old. At the school, Helga Foght taught textile printing, the weaver Franka Rasmussen taught composition, and Rolf Middelboe taught the final year.

Before Grete Ehs Østergaard went to the Netherlands for a year's traineeship at a textile company, she had already made her first sale: L.F. Foght bought her pattern 'Java' after spotting it at the school's graduation exhibition. In 1959, she established her first studio, in Trørød, but continued her cooperation with L.F. Foght. Later, she moved her studio to Malling in Jutland. Throughout her career, she designed textile printing for both home interiors and clothing.

Grete Ehs Østergaard mostly designed geometric and abstract patterns, screen printed with the dye type *indigosols*. Working with colours was a key source of inspiration to her. Her favourite colours were yellowish-green, violet and pink, a palette that continues throughout her production. Indigosol dyes were perfect for overprinting, and by layering colour shades, it was possible to achieve colours with great depth. During the 1980s, indigosols were phased out for health reasons, but because of their colour properties, Grete Ehs Østergaard continued using the type as long as possible.

Grete Ehs Østergaard (b.1938) sold several metres of her pattern 'Flet' (Weave) to the fashion shop Sohies Tøjhus in Aarhus, founded in 1969 by Birthe Pedersen. The fabric was used to make a number of dresses that were sold in the shop. During the 1970s, Grete Ehs Østergaard found it difficult to compete with all the cheap and colourful textiles that were being imported from the East, particularly from India. All the idealistic women who had established specialist crafts boutiques around the country now had to close their shops. Grete Ehs Østergaard had only limited sales from exhibitions, so overall, it was becoming difficult for textile printers to make ends meet.

**Grete Ehs Østergaard**
(b.1938)

**Wall hanging, sample,
for the Enghavegård School**
Linen, 1965

In 1965, Grete Ehs Østergaard created three large linen panels for the teachers' lounge at the Enghavegård School. She tested the design in full scale on a sample length, using both resist printing and gold-pigment printing.

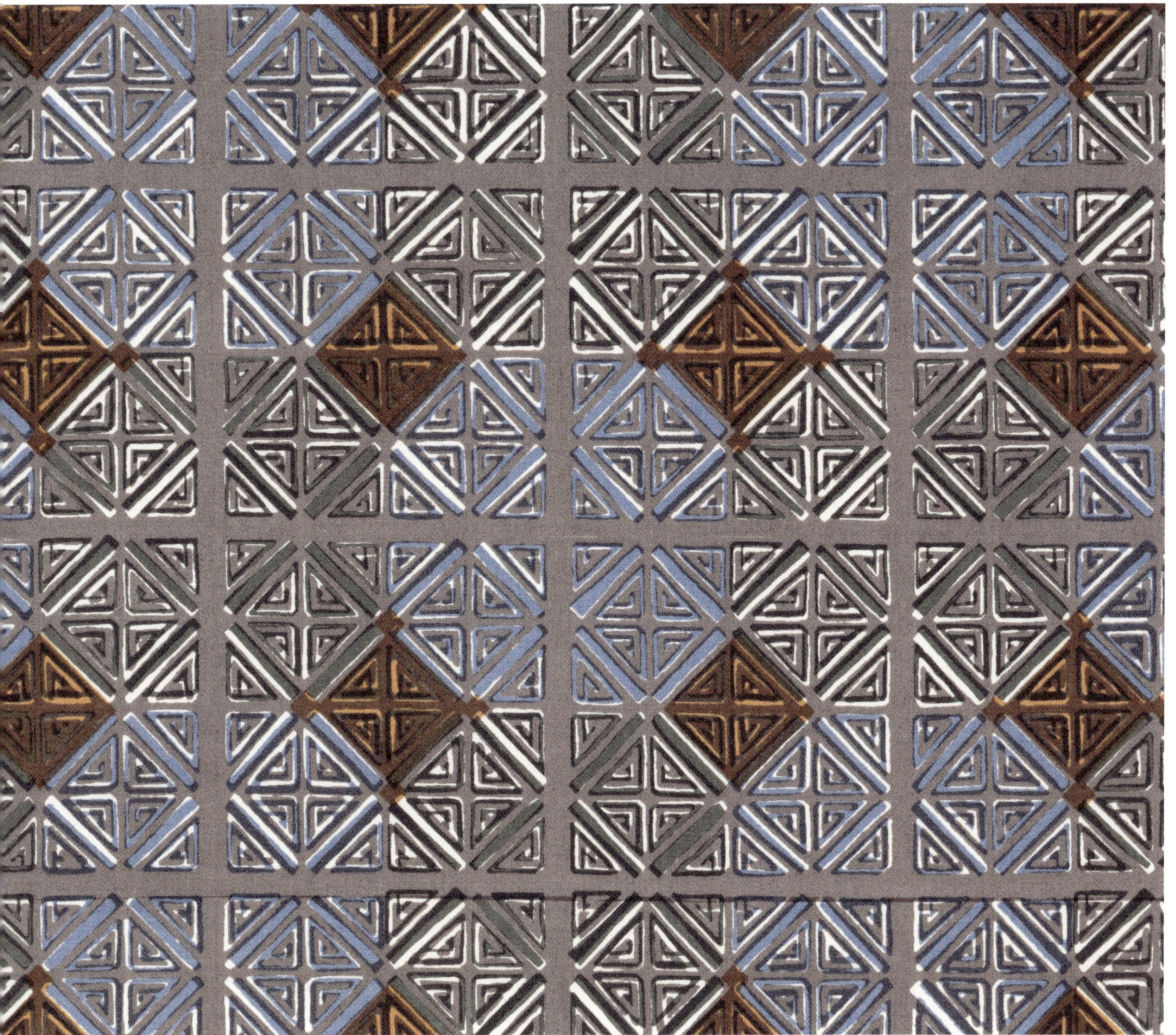

Her cooperation with L.F. Foght continued until 1964, when she designed her last pattern for the brand. In developing each new pattern, she experimented in her own studio, for example by rotating the screens 90 degrees or using overprinting, The new patterns were then presented to L.F. Foght and approved if suited for curtains. For L.F. Foght, Grete Ehs Østergaard designed 'Balloner' (Balloons), 'Escallier', 'Java', 'Labyrint' (Labyrinth), 'Løvfald' (Leaf Fall), 'Pinde' (Sticks), 'Skygger' (Shadows), 'Solhverv' (Solstice) and 'Træer' (Trees), among others. When the company closed, Grete Ehs Østergaard took over the printing screens, which she used to reprint the patterns or as part of new experiments. Some of the patterns were modified and used for fabric for dresses. She hired seamstresses to turn the textiles into dresses, which were sold in various crafts and design shops, including Den Permanente and Hanne Hansen.

From 1969 to 1980, Grete Ehs Østergaard had a series of striped clothes for toddlers sewn from cotton-jersey that was roller-printed (industrial rotogravure using rollers with engraved patterns) at the factory Martensens Fabrik in Brande. The design was a hit, in part because it marked a renewal in children's wear. Production continued for about 11 years and amounted to 3.3 tons of cotton jersey or 28,000 pieces of clothing in various models, sizes and colours. Grete Ehs Østergaard designed the models, had them tested and then sent them to a garment factory for production. Many of them were sold from the craft shop Hanne Hansen in Fiolstræde in central Copenhagen and, later, from Den Permanente. The striped cotton jersey fabric proved so popular that it was also used for women's dresses.

Grete Ehs Østergaard taught at the School of Arts and Crafts in Kolding during the 1980s. Personal experience with a child with a disability inspired her to develop educational toys in the form of games and wall hangings with interactive elements. During the 1980s, she established Det kreative Værksted (the Creative Workshop), a day school and workshop for adults with learning impairments, in Malling near Aarhus.

**Grete Ehs Østergaard**
(b.1938)

**'Labyrint' / 'Labyrinth'**
for L.F. Foght
Cotton, 1964

Grete Ehs Østergaard worked with L.F. Foght for about eight years. 'Labyrint' was one of the patterns from this collaboration that was put into industrial production.

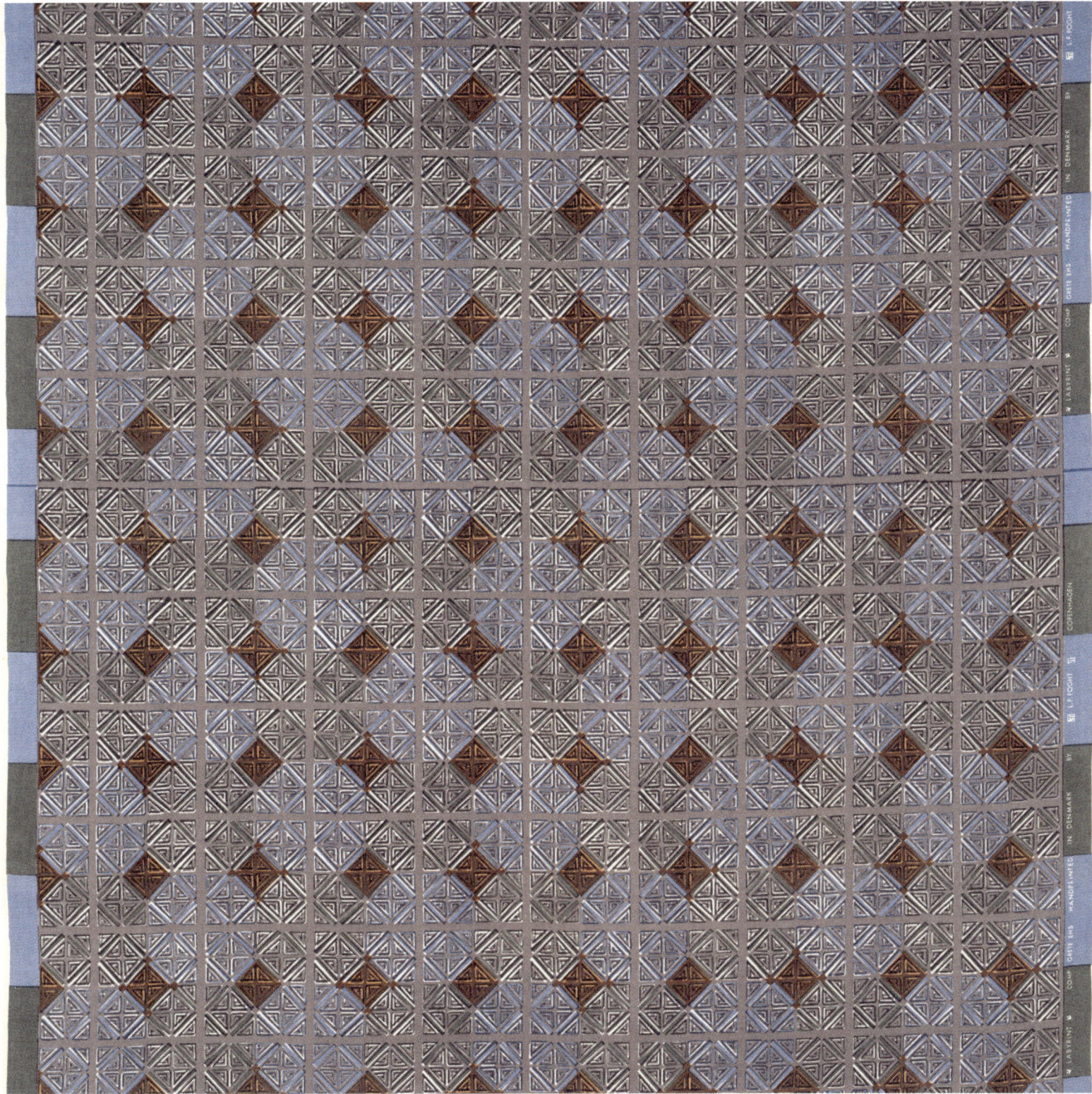

# Collaboration
# with the industry

**Egill Jacobsen**
(1910–1998)

**'Abstrakt' / 'Abstract'**
for L.F. Foght
Cotton, 1956

The painter Egill Jacobsen
designed this pattern in 1956,
when L.F. Foght worked with
a number of artists to create
textile print designs.

# Collaboration with the industry

Despite Denmark's strong tradition of solo studios and hand-printing, many textile printers worked closely with textile manufacturers. After the Second World War and the international breakthrough of Danish design, demand for Danish textiles was high, also from abroad. Several textile manufacturers saw the potential and were interested in launching an industrial production of Danish printed textiles. Many of the textile print designers partnering with industry were male architects, designers and practising artists, among them Arne Jacobsen and Axel Salto.

In 1932, the wholesale company L.F. Foght was founded by merchant Louis Frederik Foght. The company produced a variety of furnishing fabrics, including printed textile yard goods for curtains. Initially, Foght imported textiles from abroad, but currency restrictions and import regulations – during the war, a complete stop to imports – led L.F. Foght to initiate an industrial production of designs created by Danish textile makers, artists and architects. This was a shift in Danish textile production. Similar partnerships between industry and designers developed in several other European countries, for example in Sweden, which had a more developed textile industry than Denmark.

In 1939, the textile printer Helga Foght established a close collaboration with L.F. Foght, who, incidentally, was her father's cousin. Helga Foght and her later partner, Ingetoft, designed yard goods for L.F. Foght. The wholesaler also produced and sold textiles for the textile printers Gudrun Stig Aagaard and Grete Ehs Østergaard.

L.F. Foght also worked with Axel Salto. During the 1950s, the company produced printed textiles for the painters Egill Jacobsen, 'Abstrakt' (Abstract) (1956); Mogens Andersen, 'Komposition C' (Composition C) and 'Baby Dodds' (1957); and William Scharff, 'Høns' (Hens), 'Fyr' (Pine) and 'Gran' (Spruce) (1955). The fabrics were intended for home interiors. For example, one of Mogens Andersen's printed textiles was used to decorate the Copenhagen Main Library's building at Kultorvet.

As early as during the mid-1960s, L.F. Foght sought to lower the cost by dyeing the base fabric before printing or by using lower-quality fabrics. This diminished the quality of the end result and caused Grete Ehs Østergaard to give up the collaboration.

Den Blaa Fabrik was founded in 1934 by the weavers Gudrun Clemens and Brita Drewsen, mainly as a hand-weaving studio with an emphasis on upholstery fabrics, although they also produced a few printed textiles.

Marie Gudme Leth was one of the main initiators behind Dansk Kattuntrykkeri in 1935. The printing workshop was located in Copenhagen's Christianshavn district. The director of Magasin-BO, Kaj Dessau, had previously committed to carrying Leth's prints in the shop. In 1940, Marie Gudme Leth left Dansk Kattuntrykkeri over internal disagreements, which subsequently went to trial. The company continued to make prints for several decorative artists and architects, now under the name Dansk Kattuntryk.

The company Textile-Lassen was founded in 1947 by Herluf Lassen. This was both a printing workshop and a weaving mill, working mainly with Danish and Finnish designers. Herluf Lassen outsourced the work to subcontractors; for example, Finnish designs were produced in Finland. Several Danish-designed textiles

**Stig Lindberg**
(1916–1982)

**'Lystgården' / 'Country Home'**
for L.F. Foght
Cotton, 1950

The Swedish designer Stig Lindberg
designed about 30 prints for Astrid
Sampe and Nordiska Kompaniets
Textilkammare. He also designed at
least five prints for L.F. Foght. In a
similar vein to Axel Salto's pattern
based on his own ceramic vessel,
'Keramik', Stig Lindberg created a
design for a printed fabric based on
contours of his own ceramic objects,
called 'Pottery'.

**Stine Marott**
(1948-2008)

**'Jaguar'**
for Textil-Lassen
Cotton, 1971–1972

**Arne Jacobsen**
(1902–1971)

**'Foldblad'**
**/ 'White Hellebore'**
for Textil-Lassen
Cotton, 1960–1970

**Hans Christian Rasmussen**
(b.1949)

**'Cobra'**
for Textil-Lassen
51% cotton, 49% linen

Hans Christian Rasmussen graduated
from the School of Arts and Crafts in
Copenhagen in 1972 and immediately
initiated a collaboration with Textil-
Lassen. The textiles were printed at
Dansk Filmtrykkeri (Danish Film
Printing). Hans Christian Rasmussen
joined the collective workshop
Tekstil 5C. Later, during the 1990s, he
designed the fabrics 'Kaleido', 'Terna',
'Online', 'Domino', 'Triangel' (Triangle)
and 'Box' for Kvadrat.

were produced by Dansk Kattuntryk while it was located in Lille Værløse. Textil-Lassen produced fabrics for Mulle Høyrup and Stine Marott, among others. The first pattern by textile printer Hans Christian Rasmussen to go into industrial production was designed for Textil-Lassen. Textil-Lassen also put his later patterns 'Cobra', 'Net' and 'Tern' (Check) into production. Hans Christian Rasmussen later established a cooperation with Kvadrat.

There is little information available about Grautex, which produced fabrics for home interiors and clothing. According to sources, the company existed from the 1950s to the 1970s. Several Danish designers had prints produced by Grautex, including Gudrun Fisker; 'Slangestriber' (Snake Stripes); Helga Foght: 'Abstraktion' (Abstraction); Arne Jacobsen, 'Dunhammer' (Reed Mace), 'Kløver' (Clover) and 'Semicircles Petit Striped'; and Karen Schrader, 'Kavi'.

**Ingeborg Cock-Clausen**
(1929–2017)

**'Zoo'**
for Cotil
Cotton, 1957–1960

Ingeborg Cock-Clausen had an active decorative arts career from 1952 to 1968. Her collaboration with Cotil is documented in the museum's collection, including in an example of her 'Zoo' pattern. The pattern was produced in eight different colourways.

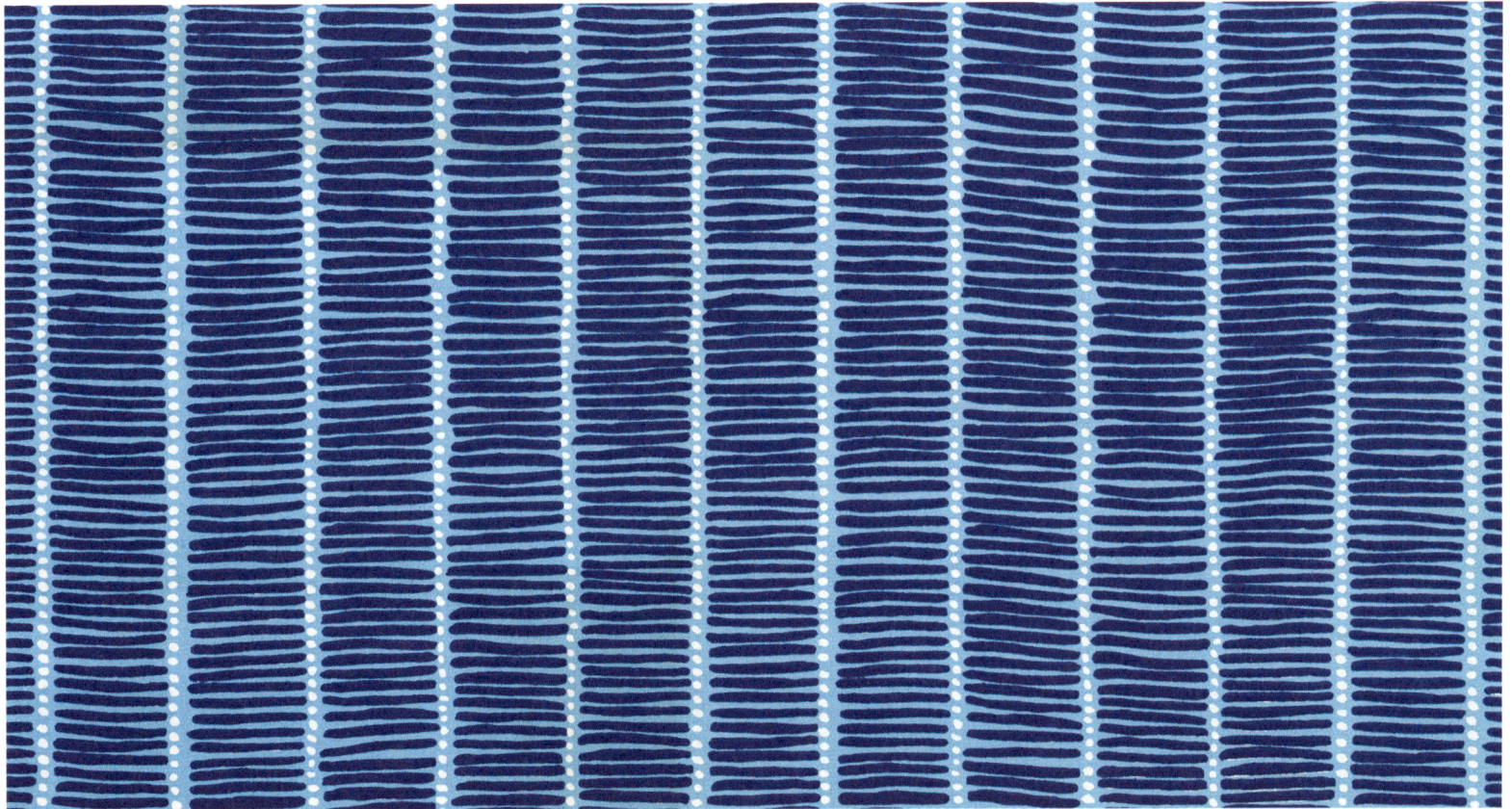

**Length of fabric in pink and green**
for Cotil
Cotton, 1956–1965

Ruth Christensen created a small
number of designs for industrially
produced yard goods. This length has
no known title, but other patterns had
names based on geographic references,
such as 'Kattegat', 'Vesterhav' (North
Sea) and 'Øresund' (the Sound).

In 1956, C. Olesen Boligtextiler – which was founded in 1892 – launched the brand Cotil: a collection of furnishing fabrics that included woven and printed curtain and upholstery fabrics as well as woven rugs and throws. The purpose of Cotil was to initiate an industrial production of furnishing textiles of high artistic and technical quality. The selection of textiles for production was handled by an independent committee comprised of members without a commercial interest in the matter. The committee members had to have day-to-day experience with design work, and together with the decorative artist, they were responsible for ensuring that the artistic qualities and technical intentions, in terms of colour, pattern, structure and quality, were expressed in the end product. Cotil played an influential role in the industrial production of textiles in Denmark, including textile printing.

**Bente Egedorf**
(b.1935)

**'Terose' / 'Tea Rose'**
for Cotil
Cotton, 1963–1964

Bente Egedorf was mostly known as a weaver of rugs and wall hangings. Her pattern 'Terose' (Tea Rose) is included in the museum's collection in four different colourways.

**Arne Jacobsen**
(1902–1971)

**'Ypsilon'**
for Cotil
Cotton, 1955–1965

Arne Jacobsen's pattern designs for Cotil were stringently geometric. Each pattern was printed in multiple colourways.

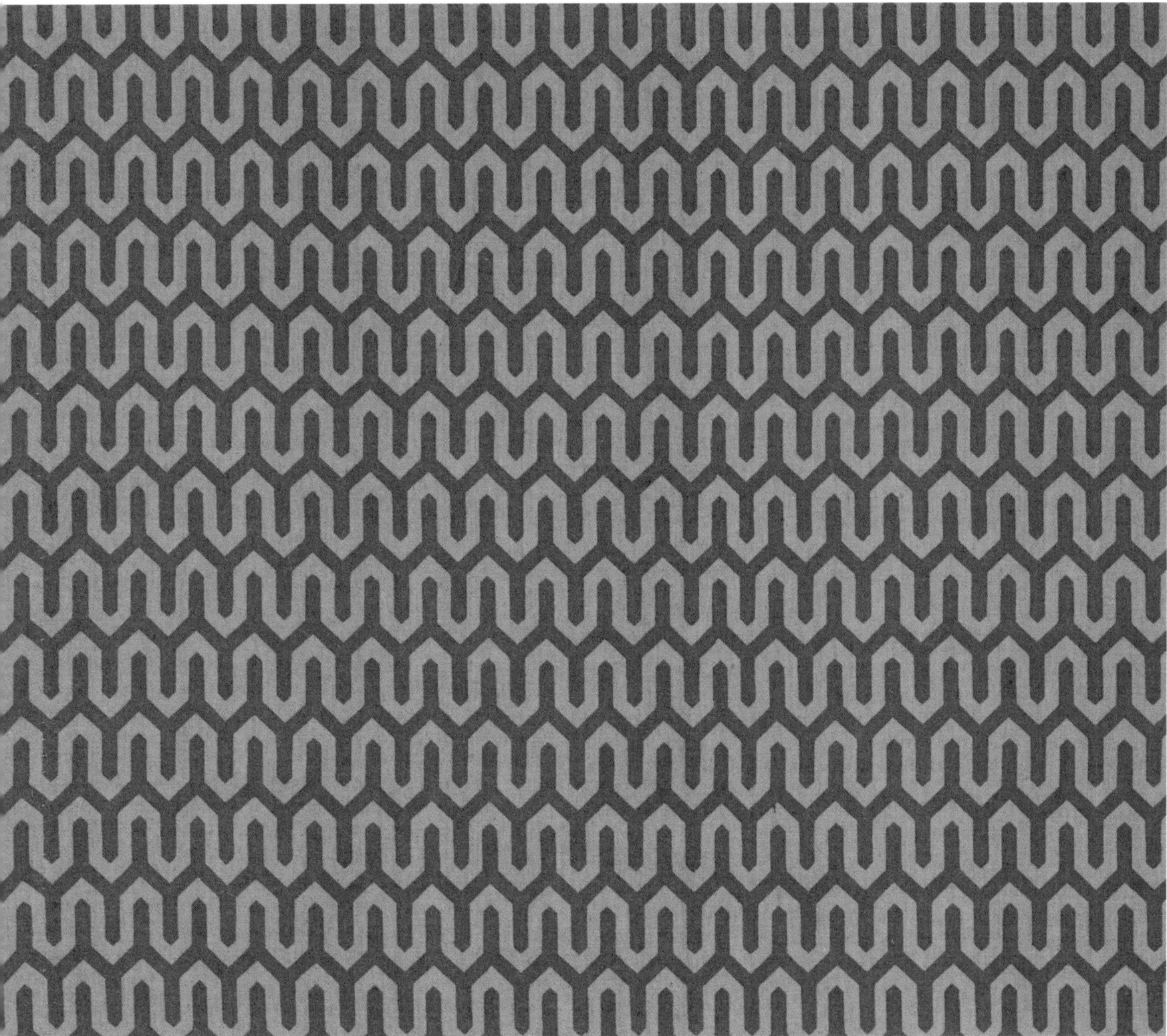

Cotil launched the largest number of printed textiles by trained textile print designers, including Ruth Christensen, Ingeborg Cock-Clausen, Susan Holm, Marie Gudme Leth and Dorte Raaschou as well as Kirsten Broen, Bente Egedorf and Mette Lac, who are less well known today. Arne Jacobsen had at least nine patterns produced by Cotil – each one in a wide range of colourways.

The collection was continually renewed and updated by the company and the independent committee. From 1956 to 1972, the committee comprised the architects Mogens Koch and Børge Mogensen, the weaver Lis Ahlmann and Director Bent Salicath. From 1975, the members were the architects Mogens Koch and Arne Karlsen and textile printer Dorte Raaschou. Cotil textiles were printed by Dansk Kattuntryk.

Percy Halling-Koch founded Unika-Væv just after the war, later founded the Halling-Koch Design Center and played a supportive role when the textile company Kvadrat was founded, in 1968. The main initiators behind Kvadrat were two former salespeople from Unika-Væv, Poul Byriel and Erling Rasmussen. Unika-Væv had previously advertised textile prints and had worked with the textile printers Ruth Hull and Rolf Middelboe and with the artist, designer and architect Gunnar Aagaard Andersen.

**Susan Holm**
(1937–2020)

**'Sukatka'**
for Cotil
Cotton, 1971

In 1963–1964, Susan Holm volunteered for six months at Helga Foght's workshop, and the following year, in 1965, she established her own. In addition to designing for Cotil, she printed one-off textiles and created artisanal clothing.

Today, Kvadrat is one of the largest textile manufacturers in Northern Europe, with a particular emphasis on products for public setting and environments with heightened requirements to wear and fire resistance. During the 1980s, Kvadrat produced printed textiles in collaboration with the textile printer Anne Gry, the architect, visual artist and designer Ole Kortzau, the painter Tom Krøjer, the American graphic artist Ross Littell, the painter Niels Nedergaard, the painter, graphic artist and designer Finn Sködt and the textile printer Grete Ehs Østergaard. During the 1990s, the company worked with the textile printers Nina Ferlov, Helle Graabæk and Charlotte Houmann, the painter Arne L. Hansen, the textile printers Hans Christian Rasmussen and Vibeke Riisberg, the weaver Naja Salto and the painter Ole Schwalbe.

**Finn Sködt**
(1944–2019)

**'Babylon'**
for Kvadrat
Cotton, 1980–1987

Brushstrokes and pencil hatchings were favoured motifs during the 1980s. In 'Babylon', Finn Sködt used hatching in fiery lines. In enlarged form, the lines are elegantly worked into a pattern repeat.

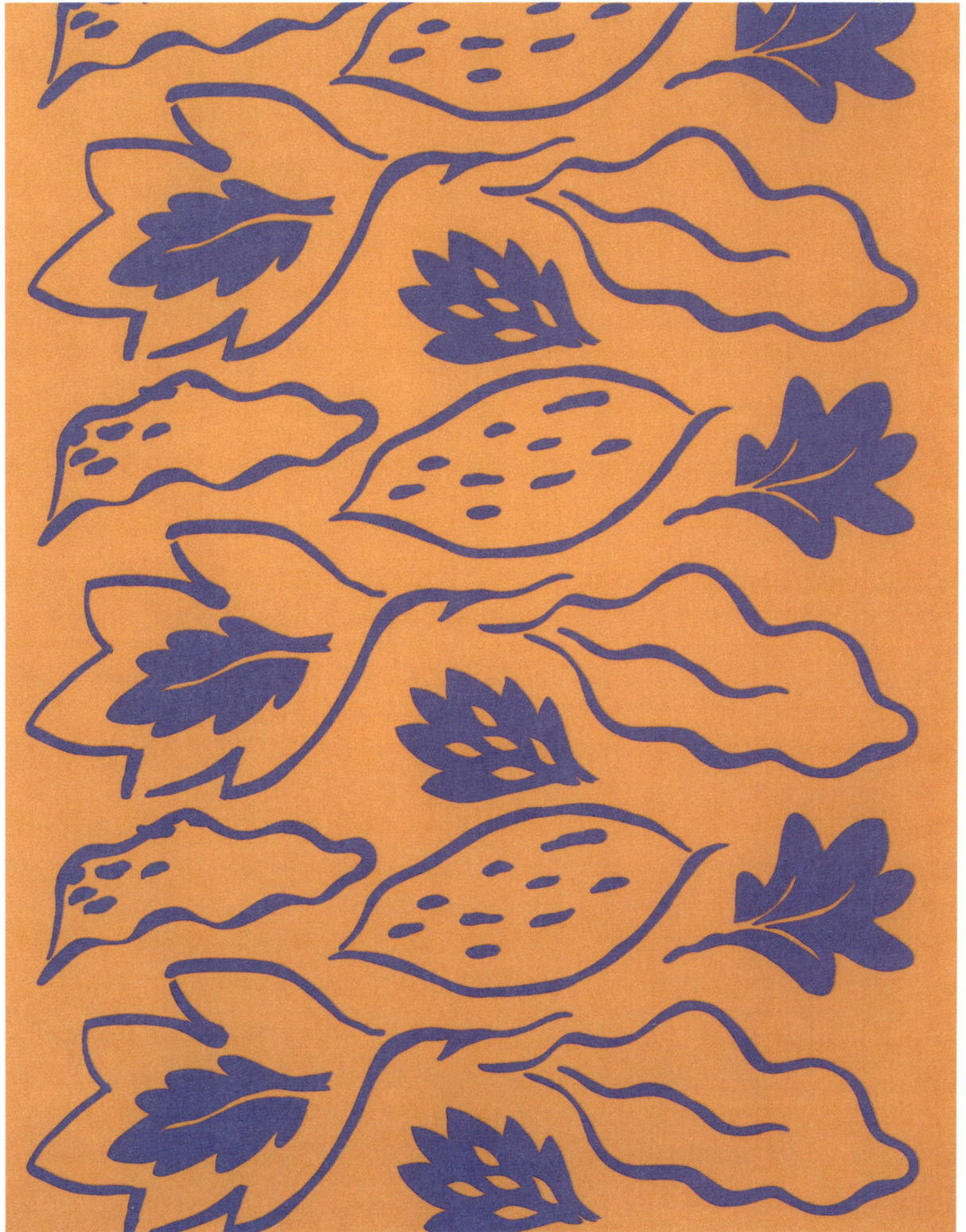

**Anne Gry**
(b.1943)

**'Padova'**
for Kvadrat
Trevira, 1990–2003

Anne Gry worked for Kvadrat as a
freelance designer from 1972. From
1971 to 1978, she worked with Hanne
Hansen in Fiolstræde on furnishing
fabrics and with clothing designer Tora
Winther on fabrics for clothing.

**Ross Littell**
(1924–2000)

**'Fold Up Multi'**
for Kvadrat
Cotton, 1985–1986

The American textile and furniture
designer Ross Littell, who lived in
Denmark for some time, was a big
admirer of Scandinavian design. His
textiles for Kvadrat have a geometric
and graphic expression.

**Ole Kortzau**
(b.1939)

**'Moves'**
for Kvadrat
Cotton/viscose, 1980–1986

The print patterns 'Moves' and 'Waves' – the same pattern but with multi-colour lines on a light-coloured background – from Kvadrat were among the most popular curtain fabrics for public institutions during the 1980s.

**Ole Kortzau**
(b.1939)

**'Holiday'**
for Kvadrat
Cotton, 1980–1986

This pattern is typical of its time, with bright, clear colours and naive images signalling summer and sun.

**Niels Nedergaard**
(1944–1987)

**'Musalas'**
for Kvadrat
Cotton, 1984–1986

The painter Niels Nedergaard's design for Kvadrat was influenced by Islamic geometric ornamentation, inspired by his stay in Cairo from 1979 to 1986.

**Finn Sködt**
(1944–2019)

**'Crunch'**
for Kvadrat
Cotton, 1980–1986

The painter, graphic artist and designer Finn Sködt created several patterns for Kvadrat, designed for large, decorative window coverings. His 1980s patterns were playful, with an almost naive expression, and printed in bright colours.

133

**Arne L. Hansen**
(1921–2009)

**'Colour Tone'**
for Kvadrat
Cotton, circa 1990

The painter Arne L. Hansen designed
many decorative projects for public
buildings and churches around
Denmark.

Designers and textile printers often worked with more than one company; the partnerships were not necessarily exclusive. For example, Grete Ehs Østergaard's designs were printed both by L.F. Foght and Kvadrat, and Arne Jacobsen's textiles were printed by Cotil, Textil-Lassen and Grautex. Even though Helga Foght was related to L.F. Foght and had yard goods in production under the brand, some of her patterns were printed under the Grautex brand.

**Vibeke Riisberg**
(b.1951)

**'Vibration'**
Cotton, 1990–1992

'Vibration' is a further development, in collaboration with Kvadrat, of hand-printed textiles from the exhibition *7 Illusioner* (7 Illusions) at the Museum of Decorative Art.

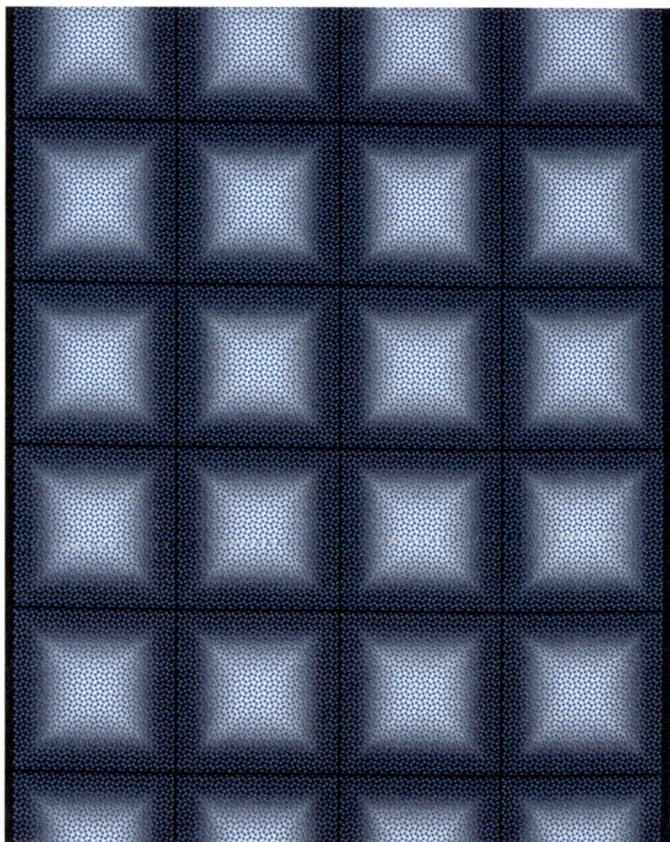

**Ole Schwalbe**
(1929–1990)

**'Geometry I'**
for Kvadrat
Cotton, 1990

Ole Schwalbe was a self-taught artist. He worked with concrete realism and geometric shapes. Originally a trained lithographer, he liked to experiment with various expressive modes on the two-dimensional surface.

**Verner Panton**
(1926–1998)

**'Mira Spectrum'**
for Mira-X
Cotton, 1969–1971

Among other design activities, the
Danish architect Verner Panton
created entire interiors, including
furniture, lamps, textiles and more.
This textile was part of the collection
Decor 1 for the German company
Mira-X.

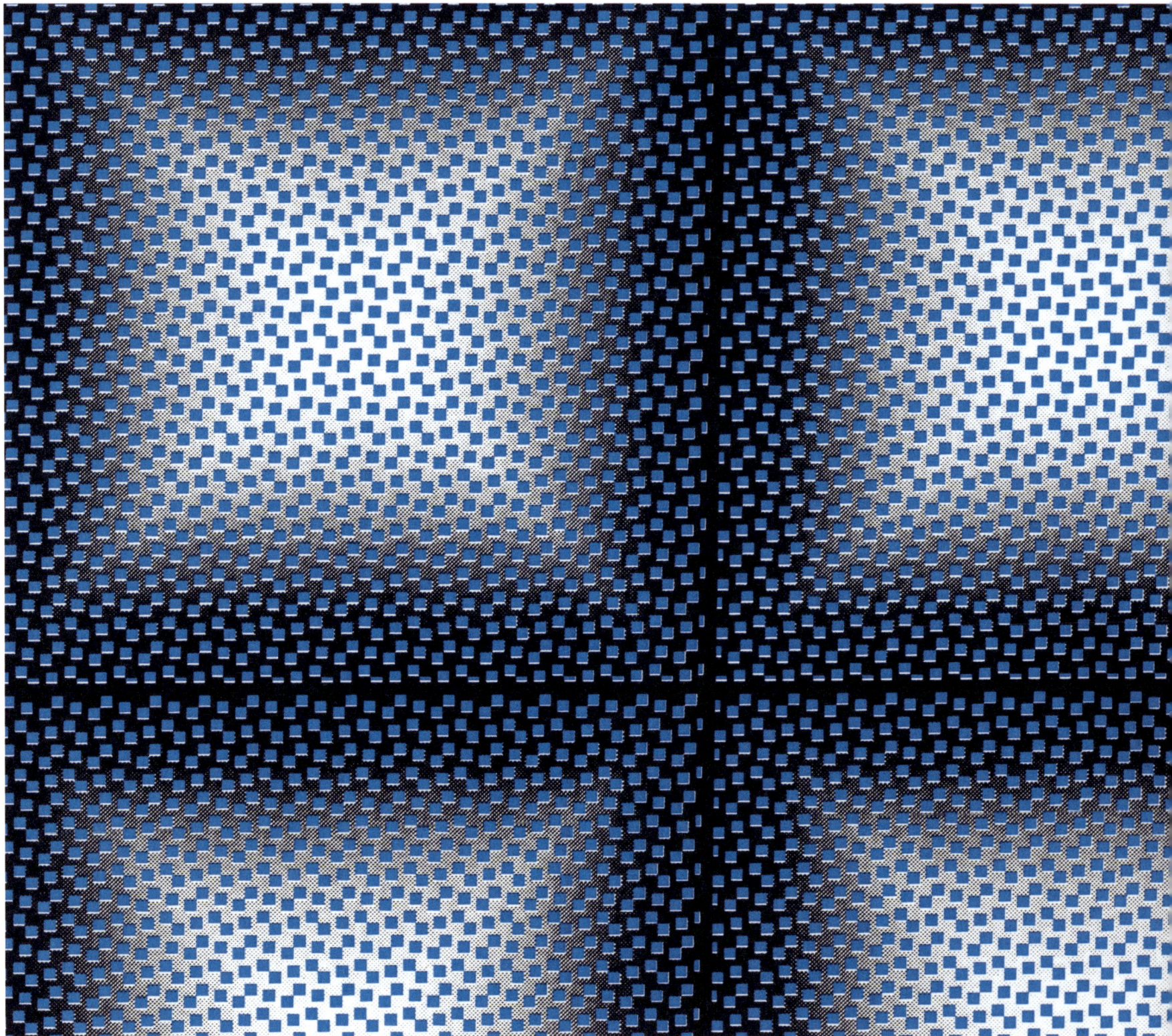

# Artisanal
# clothing

**Dorte Raaschou**
(1929–2011)

**Summer dress with black straps**
Silk, circa 1960

Dorte Raaschou printed many silk textiles that were used to make dresses.

# Artisanal clothing

From the 1950s, many Danish textile artists, weavers as well as textile printers, created fabrics intended for clothing. These popular 'artisanal clothes' were often printed (or woven), designed and sewn by a textile designer, sometimes in a collaboration with a clothing designer. In 1962, when Dorte Raaschou received the Cotil Prize, a prize exhibition at the Den Permanente featured dresses made of some of her printed textiles. The designer Astrid Fog, whose portfolio included clothing design, both couture and ready-to-wear, sewed the models for the exhibition.

Artisanal clothing was sold from a number of boutiques and larger shops, including Den Permanente and Haandarbejdets Fremme shops. In 1966, Illums Bolighus opened a shop-in-shop for artisanal clothes. Other textile printers, besides Dorte Raaschou, also worked with clothing design, including Ruth Christensen, Anne Gry, Susan Holm and Ruth Hull.

The production process might vary a great deal among different makers, just as there was considerable variation in how many pieces each maker produced of a given model. Many designs were one-offs. Sometimes, the textile printer would only print on the parts of the textile that were included in the finished piece. This saved on ink or dye and could also be used to position the print just right in the finished item, so-called print-to-measure. From the 1950s to the 1970s, almost all artisanal clothes were made of natural materials such as wool, silk, linen or cotton.

One of the first public presentations of this type of artisanal clothing was probably an exhibition at the workshop gallery Studio Schrader in Niels Hemmingsens Gade 10 in central Copenhagen in 1952. The exhibition showed clothes created in a collaboration between textile printers and clothing designers. It featured works by several leading textile printers, including Ruth Christensen, Ruth Hull, Mulle Høyrup, Ingermarie Ostenfeld, Bodil Oxenvad, Dorte Raaschou, Karen Schrader and Aase Seidler. The exhibition was followed up by a fashion show with 86 models at the Karnappen restaurant. Several exhibitions and shows followed, both at Den Permanente and in Haandarbejdets Fremme shops.

**Bodil Oxenvad**
(1915–2011)

**Long evening gown, 'Solskin i Græs' / 'Sunshine on Grass'**
Tulle, taffeta, duveteen, 1952

The outer layer of the skirt is made of tulle featuring a pattern made of multiple layered overprints. The dress was created for an exhibition at Haandarbejdets Fremme in 1952 and later donated to the museum by Bodil Oxenvad.

**Ruth Hull**
(1912–1996)

**Dress with belt**
Cotton, 1963–1964

Heavy cotton textile
with a painted pattern.

**Bodil Bødtker-Næss**
(1942-1988),
print design and execution

**Printed dress from
Den Permanente**
Cotton, 1965

Bodil Bødtker-Næss originally
trained as a textile printer but later
became known for her woven wall
hangings. The dress was bought
at Den Permanente and worn as
a wedding gown.

**Karen Schrader**
(1898–1986)

**Girl's dress in batik**
Silk, 1950–1960

Karen Schrader worked with batik
during the early part of her career.
However, this dress for a child was
made later.

**Dorte Raaschou**
(1929–2011)

**Dress with 'Strega' pattern**
Raw silk, circa 1960

'Strega' was one of the patterns that
Cotil put into industrial production.
Here, Dorte Raaschou has printed her
own pattern on silk, probably in her
own workshop.

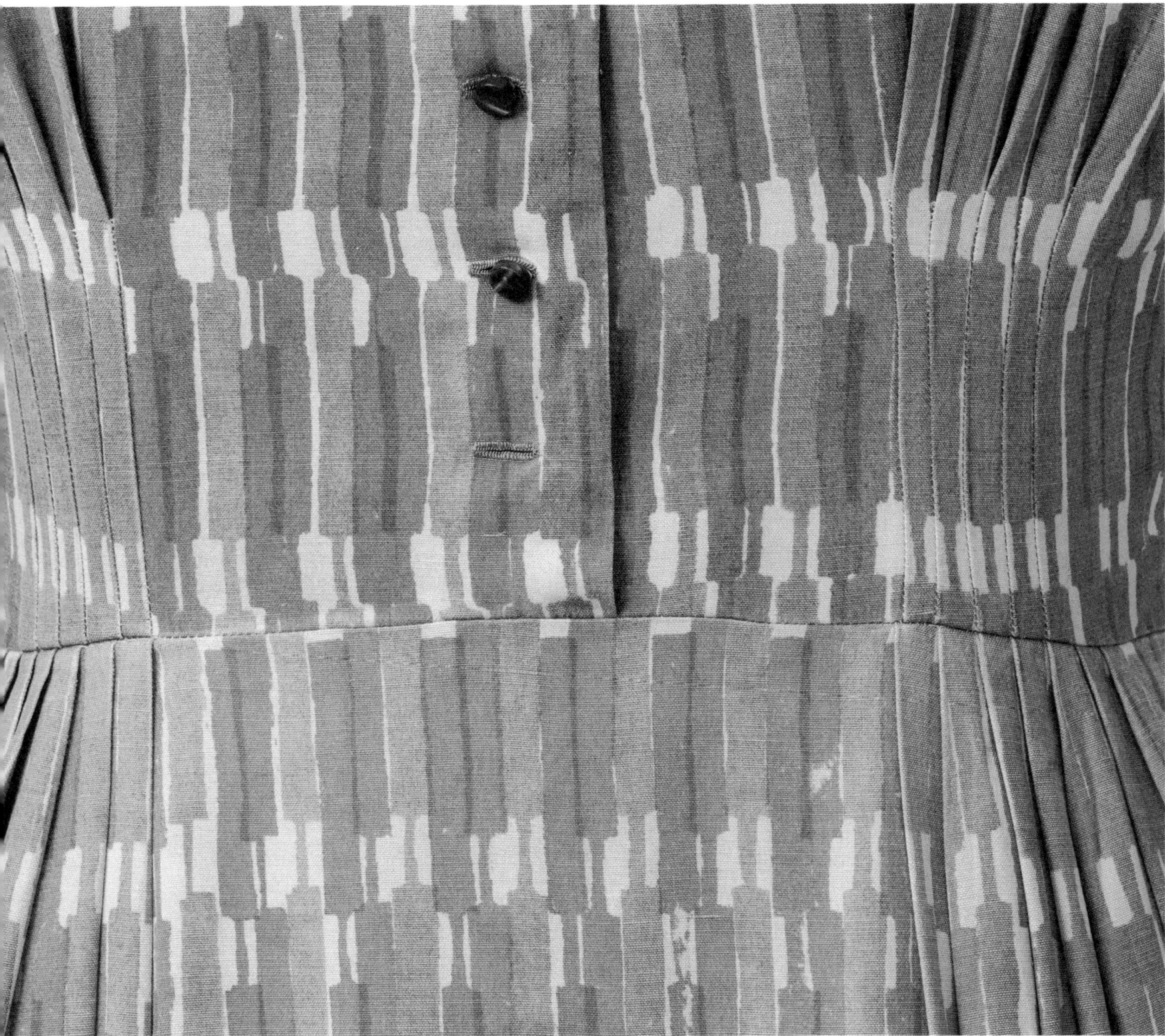

**Hanne Backhaus**
(b.1942),
print design

**Pia Hedegaard**
(1932–2016),
clothing design

**Kimono jacket and shorts**
Cotton, 1980s

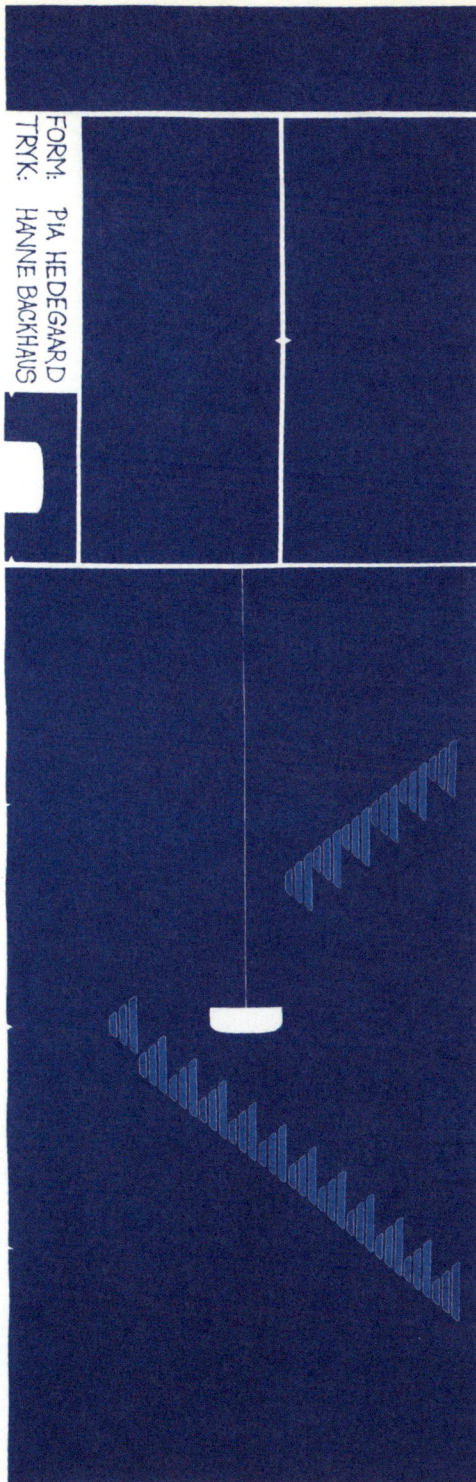

FORM: PIA HEDEGAARD
TRYK: HANNE BACKHAUS

During the late 1960s and the 1970s, the distinction between artisanal clothing and mass-produced fashion was highlighted not only by the practising decorative artists but also in the press. Artisanal clothes became a political statement, signalling that the wearer was not a follower of commercial fashion. The Charlottenborg art centre and the Louisiana Museum of Modern Art opened their doors to runway shows, which naturally added to the clothes' cultural cachet. Marimekko was a leading brand, even though its clothes were mass-produced, not one-offs. Artisanal clothes were not cheap, but neither were Marimekko dresses at the time.

In addition to the shops mentioned above, artisanal clothes were also sold by Hanne Hansen, who opened a shop in Fiolstræde in 1966 and soon established a collaboration with decorative artists and craft studios. The shop held small solo exhibitions and had beautiful window displays of Danish craft products. For a number of years during the 1970s, the textile printer Anne Gry and clothing designer Tora Winther designed and printed two annual bespoke collections for the shop.

**Hanne Backhaus**
(b.1942),
print design

**Pia Hedegaard**
(1932–2016),
clothing design

**Length of fabric with printed pattern, 'print to measure'**
Cotton, 1980s

This length of fabric shows the pattern laid out and printed in blue for a kimono jacket. The customer would then simply cut it out of the fabric as indicated by the print and sew it themselves. In French, the technique is known as 'à la disposition', and there are known examples dating back to the 18th century with several different clothing items and with other decoration methods besides textile printing.

**Inge Ingetoft**
(1929–1996)

**Wrap dress, 'Prikker' / 'Dots'**
Cotton, 1978

In addition to furnishing fabrics, Inge Ingetoft printed fabrics for a range of other purposes, including clothing.

**Susan Holm**
(1937–2020)

**Kimono**
Cotton batiste, 1989

Susan Holm had a fairly large
production of artisanal clothing
during her career. In order to achieve
more control over the cutting of the
clothes, she took additional training
at Københavns Tilskærerakademi
(Copenhagen Pattern Cutting
Academy) in 1968.

**Ruth Hull**
(1912–1996)

**Summer dress**
Silk, 1960–1961

The motif of this silk dress was
created using a combination of
painting, colour etching and resist
block printing. There is no record
of who cut and sewed the dress.

**Rune Sckerl**
(1939–2017)

**Length of fabric**
Silk, 1989

Jette and Rune Sckerl met at the School of Arts and Crafts in Copenhagen. They both graduated in 1961. From 1964, they developed their own company making artisanal clothes in the town of Hundslund between Horsens and Odder. He designed and printed the patterns, and she designed the clothing. In addition to yard goods for clothing, Rune Sckerl also printed decorative fabrics.

**Anne Gry**
(b.1943),
print design

**Tora Winther**
(b.1946),
dress design

**Long dress with halterneck**
Cotton, 1970s

During most of the 1970s, textile
printer Anne Gry and clothing
designer Tora Winther created limited
dress collections for Hanne Hansen's
crafts shop in Fiolstræde in central
Copenhagen.

**Marie Gudme Leth**
(1895–1997),
textile design

**Short shirt dress,
'Mariati med Hvid Udsparing'
/ 'Mariati with White Masking'**
from 1958
Cotton, 1970s

'Mariati med Hvid Udsparing' was
one of the patterns by Marie Gudme
Leth that was industrially produced
for Cotil during the 1960s after she
had stopped printing in her own
workshop. The dress/shirt was sewn
by a private individual from a length
of fabric from Cotil.

**Vibeke Riisberg**
(b.1951),
print design

**Thomas Winkler**
(b.1963),
dress design

**T-shirt and skirt**
Viscose jersey, cotton, 1998

Vibeke Riisberg printed the fabric
for the skirt in her own workshop.

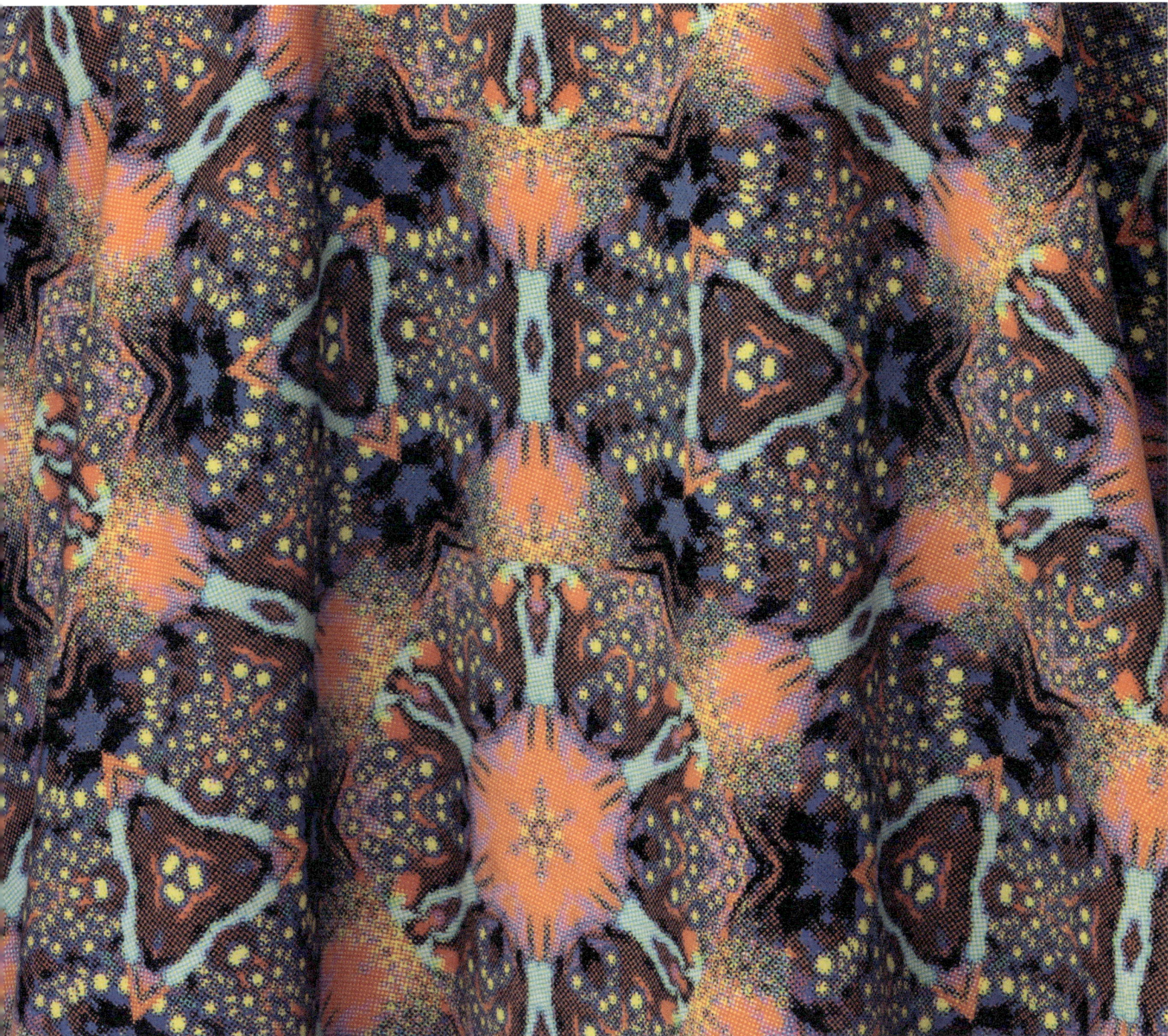

**Anne Fabricius Møller**
(b.1959),
print design

**Thomas Winkler**
(b.1963),
dress design

**Half-length dress**
Linen, 1989

This dress was made in a collaboration between Anne Fabricius Møller and Thomas Winkler. In order to achieve the patination effect, Anne Fabricius Møller printed on both sides of the linen fabric.

# Sales channels for printed textiles and artisanal clothes

# Sales channels for printed textiles and artisanal clothes

Partnering with industry was essential for the ability of textile printers to market their products to a wider audience, but having proper sales channels was equally important.

Magasin-BO was founded by Kaj Dessau. The home design shop on Strøget in central Copenhagen opened on 1 December 1928. The venue served both as a shop and as a gallery. During its 13-year existence, it played a significant role for the breakthrough of functionalist home design, with bright, airy presentations of industrial and crafts products. As mentioned earlier, Magasin-BO was key in facilitating Marie Gudme Leth's breakthrough.

In 1941, Magasin-BO had to close, but a few months later, the shop was taken over by Illums Bolighus, which maintained a similar selection of products. For example, Marie Gudme Leth's textiles, which were now produced in her own workshop, were sold at Illums Bolighus. Magasin-BO and, from 1941, its successor, Illums Bolighus, was a key influence on the view of modern home design among the affluent middle classes for many years to come.

Selskabet til Haandarbejdets Fremme, which was founded in 1928, aimed to drive renewal in Danish textile art by promoting beautiful and artistic high-quality needlework and textile crafts through new models and patterns designed by leading contemporary artists. As part of this overall effort, the association also aimed to provide sales channels for decorative artists and makers by opening shops in several towns and cities around Denmark.

Den Permanente, which was located in the 'Vesterport' building on Vesterbrogade in central Copenhagen, opened in December 1931. Most Danes knew Den Permanente as an exhibition venue and shop. In fact, Den Permanente was a private association and a collective sales organization. Its purpose was to provide and maintain a permanent exhibition venue in Copenhagen. Den Permanente presented and sold its members' works within all genres of crafts and decorative arts. Like Selskabet til Haandarbejdets Fremme, Den Permanente had a juried selection process to maintain a high level of quality. The main purpose was to display craft products made in small workshops that did not have their own shop or exhibition space.

In addition to special exhibitions in its own space, Den Permanente also organized and participated in many large travelling exhibitions abroad and in the Milan Triennials during the 1950s together with the association Danish Arts and Crafts and Industrial Design. This international exposure enhanced the standing of Danish crafts and decorative arts abroad and naturally helped increase exports for Den Permanente. The association behind Den Permanente disbanded in 1981.

As mentioned earlier, in addition to Hanne Hansen's shop in Fiolstræde, many larger towns and cities had several small shops that sold hand-crafted products. During the 1970s, craft collectives were established that ran their own independent shops.

1970 to 2020

**Mulle Høyrup**
(1913–1992)

**'Flammer' / 'Flames'**
Silk, 1973

Mulle Høyrup established her own
studio in 1944, while she was attending
the School of Arts and Crafts, where
she studied from 1944 to 1946. She
launched a school for experimental
textile printing in 1965. Mulle Høyrup's
practice included both decoration
projects and artisanal clothes.
This length of silk was created using
a combination of block printing,
screen printing and painting.

# 1970 to 2020

The 1970s and 1980s were a difficult time for the Danish textile industry. Several manufacturers closed, as the import of fabrics increased, making the domestic production of yard goods unsustainable for most companies. Several large shops also closed, and many textile printers established collective workshops and boutiques. During this time, political and social views and opinions influenced both imagery and working methods.

Patterns ranged from geometric and graphically clarified designs in bright colours to shading, brushstrokes and soft transitions. Many textile printers had a free and artistic expression, without repeats, and exhibitions became an important sales channel.

During the 1980s and 1990s, a new textile printing technology was developed. The combination of computer-aided design programs and digital printing created new possibilities for visual design development.

The styles were varied and colourful. Meanwhile, globalization was enabling more textile printers to bring their textiles and patterns to a wider international audience. As a consequence of globalization and technological innovation, knowledge about the traditional craft and its possibilities gradually began to slip away.

A few textile makers created large-scale decoration and interior design projects on commission from architects and building clients. Others created textiles for costumes and stage design. Textile printers searched for new ways of making a living, as society was changing. While the boundaries between art, crafts and design were falling away, textile printing during the 1990s and 2000s moved toward a more artistic expression, as did other craft disciplines.

The textile company Kvadrat maintained the tradition of partnering with artists and textile artists. Kvadrat adapted their proposals to be produced in materials, qualities and colours that appealed to new markets in Denmark and abroad.

Today, textile printing spans many styles and diverse expressions. Some Danish textile printers, for example Lisbet Friis, Bitten Hegelund, Dorte Østergaard Jacobsen, Anne Fabricius Møller, Vibeke Rohland and Louise Sass, are strong exponents of a new approach to the craft, using images, colour shades and lighting to create immersive spatial experiences.

The traditional Danish workshop or studio culture is entering a new phase, as crafts traditions, hands-on experience, artistic intuition and knowledge of chemistry are combined with modern technology. Several textile printers work in series, and the process is reflected in the aesthetic expression. The textile expression is developed in a layered structure that brings depth and three-dimensionality to the textile.

The museum's 2025 exhibition *The Power of Print* includes textile prints by a group of eight women textile printers and artists from the current art and design scene, several of whom are already represented in the museum's collection. Josefina Enevold, Lisbet Friis, Bitten Hegelund, Else Borup Kallesøe, Anne Fabricius Møller, Liv Marie Rømer, Trine Tronhjem and Janne Wendt created new bespoke pieces for the exhibition.

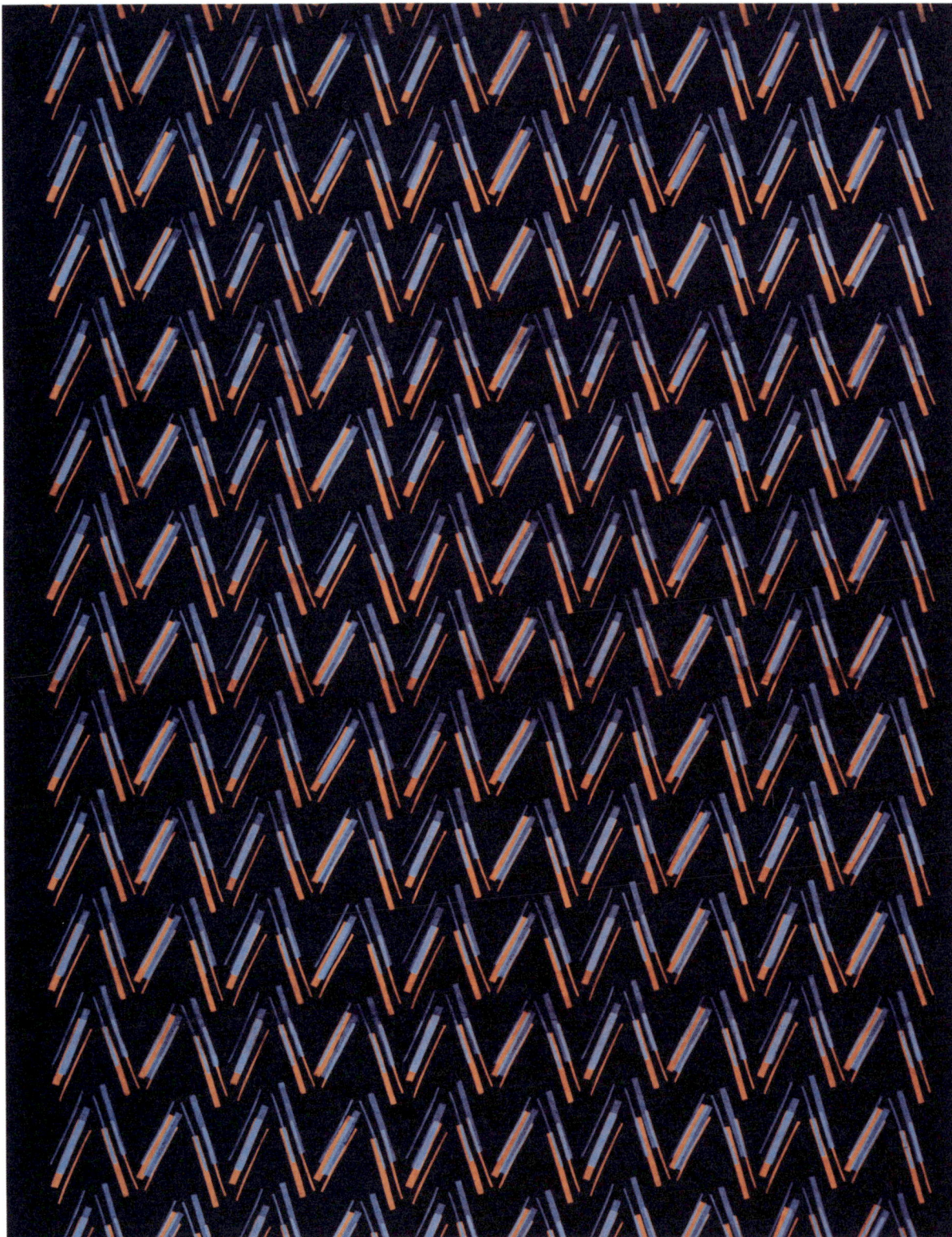

**Hanne Backhaus**
(b.1942)

**'Nat i Ramløse' / 'Night in Ramløse'**
Cotton, 1986

The textile printer Hanne Backhaus graduated from the School of Arts and Crafts in Copenhagen in 1963. That same year, she established her own studio. Before then, she had spent a year working in Marie Gudme Leth's studio. The two formed a friendship that lasted until Marie Gudme Leth's death, in 1997. Hanne Backhaus was a cofounder of the collective workshop 'Sirenerne' and later of the shop 'Blå Form' (Blue Form) in Rådhusstræde in central Copenhagen.

**Helle Abild**
(b.1964)

**'Y2K Quilt'**
Cotton, 1999

Helle Abild was one of the first Danish textile designers to use computer drawing programs. This pattern was developed using a kaleidoscopic repetition of a single design element based on 17 prototypes. Digital print.

**Lisette Kampmann**
(1924–2022)

**Wall hanging**
Cotton, 1974–1977

Lisette Kampmann, who was self-taught, worked with yard goods, compositions for one-off wall hangings, serially produced clothing and even preprinted cardboard sheets for cutting on behalf of the World Wildlife Foundation. She was politically engaged, as reflected in the titles of some of her works. She was a member of the collective workshop 'Sirenerne' (the Sirens).

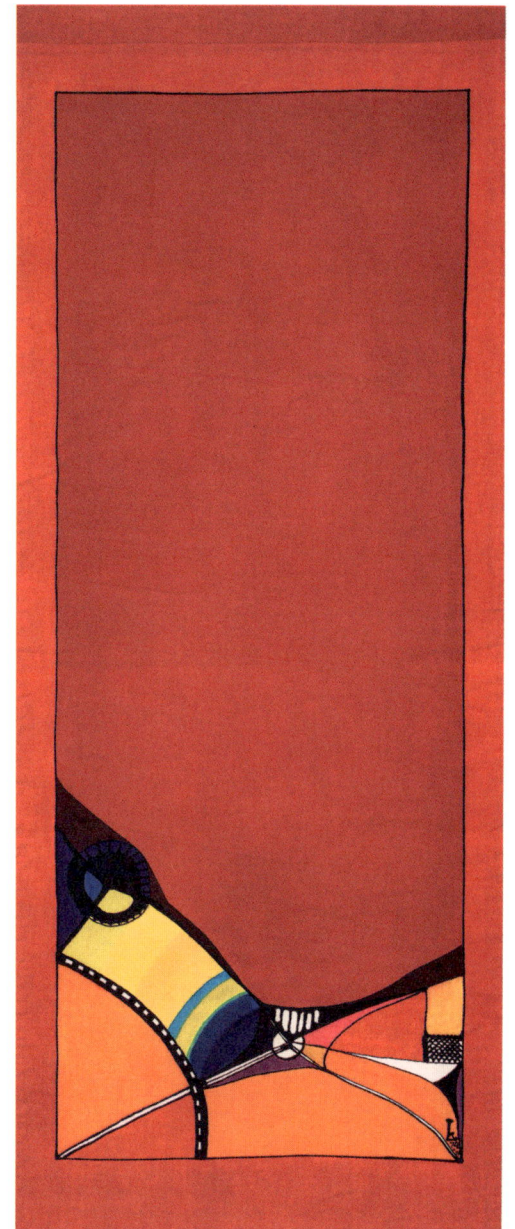

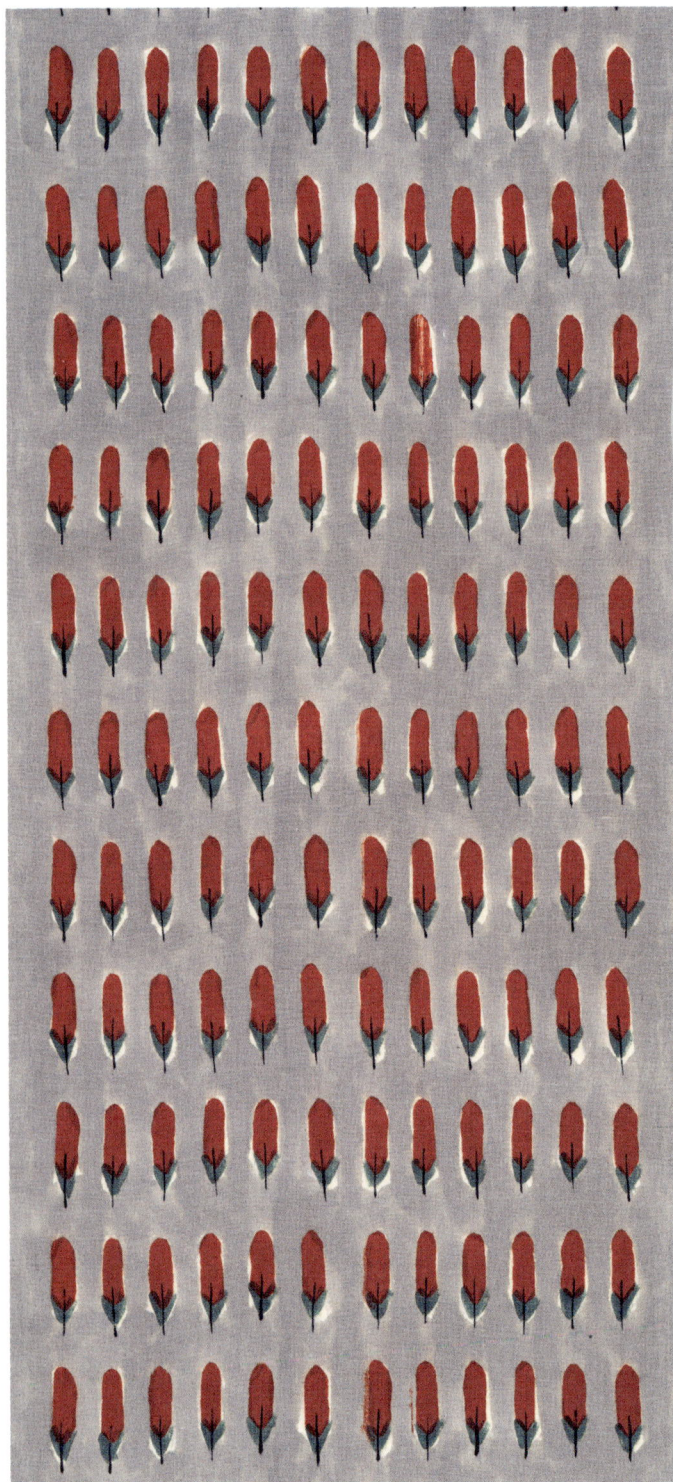

**Johanne Heide**
(b.1959)

**'Fjer' / 'Feathers'**
Linen, 1984

Johanne Heide graduated from
the School of Arts and Crafts in
Copenhagen in 1982, the same year
that she established her workshop
Tryk 15 (Print 15) with a group of other
textile printers. This length of fabric
was used for the opening exhibition
at the crafts gallery K – Galleri for
Kunsthåndværk' (C – Galleri for Crafts)
in Kompagnistræde.

**Ruth Fabricius**
(b.1957)

**Length of fabric**
Linen, 1988

The fabric was inspired by medieval
ornamentation from the Cluny
museum in Paris. In 1990, Ruth
Fabricius cofounded the company
Kurage with Jesper Gundersen.
In 2005, Kurage became part of
the Fisher Group. They both create
designs for the Fisher Group today.

**Dorte Østergaard Jakobsen**
(b.1957)

**Ruth Fabricius**
(b.1957)

**Length of fabric**
Silk, 1984–1987

From 1984 to 1987, the two textile
printers had a joint workshop which
they called 'Emballage' (Packaging).
This fabric probably dates from
that period.

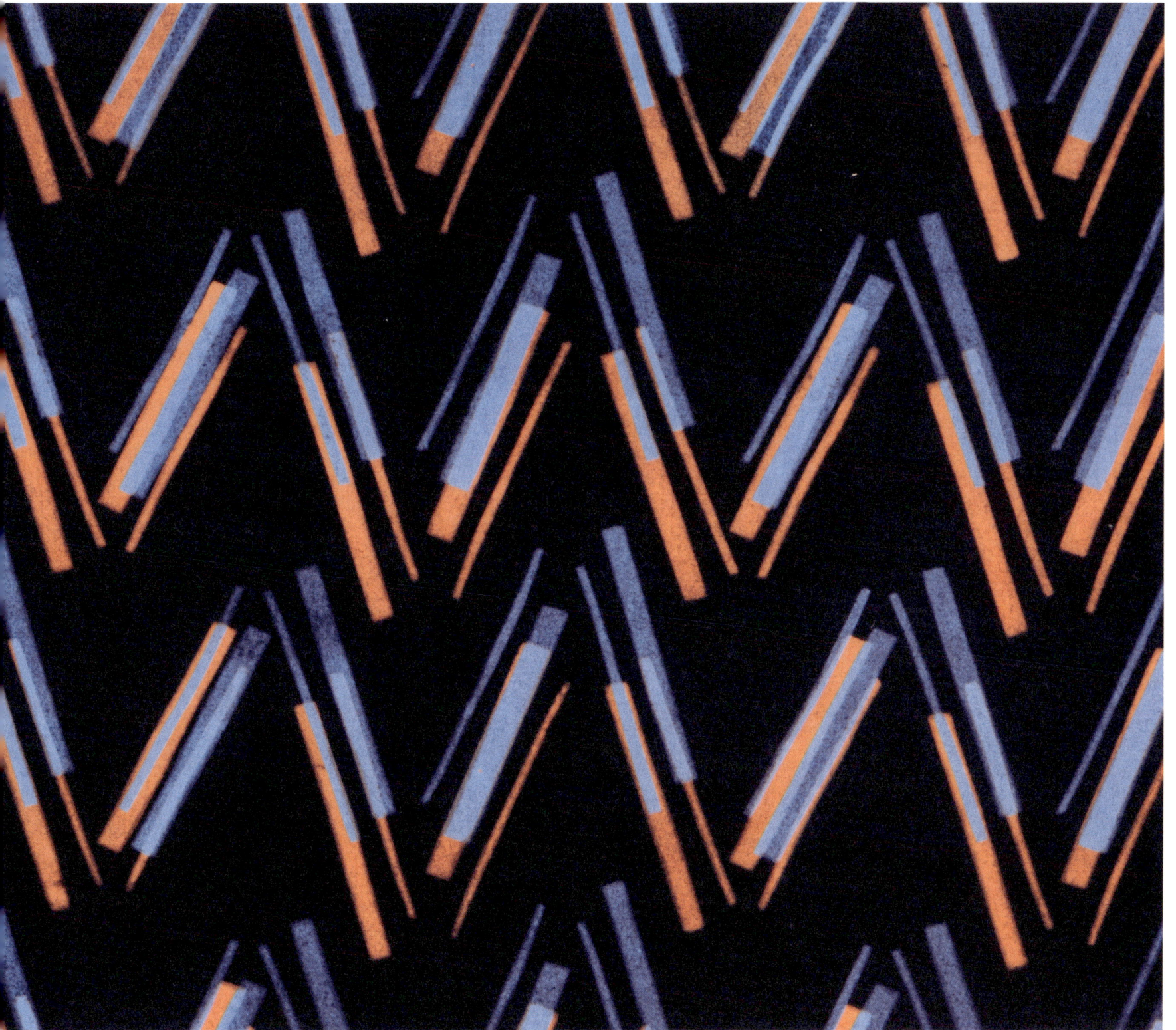

**Ursula Krabbe**
(b.1957)

**Length of fabric**
Silk, 1985

After her graduation from the School
of Arts and Crafts in Copenhagen
in 1981, Ursula Krabbe established
a joint studio, Tryk 15 (Print 15),
together with the textile printer
Johanne Heide, among others. This
length of fabric was created for the
exhibition *Museumsinspirationer*
(Museum Inspirations) at Kalundborg
og Omegns Museer (Museums of
Kalundborg and Environs) in 1985.

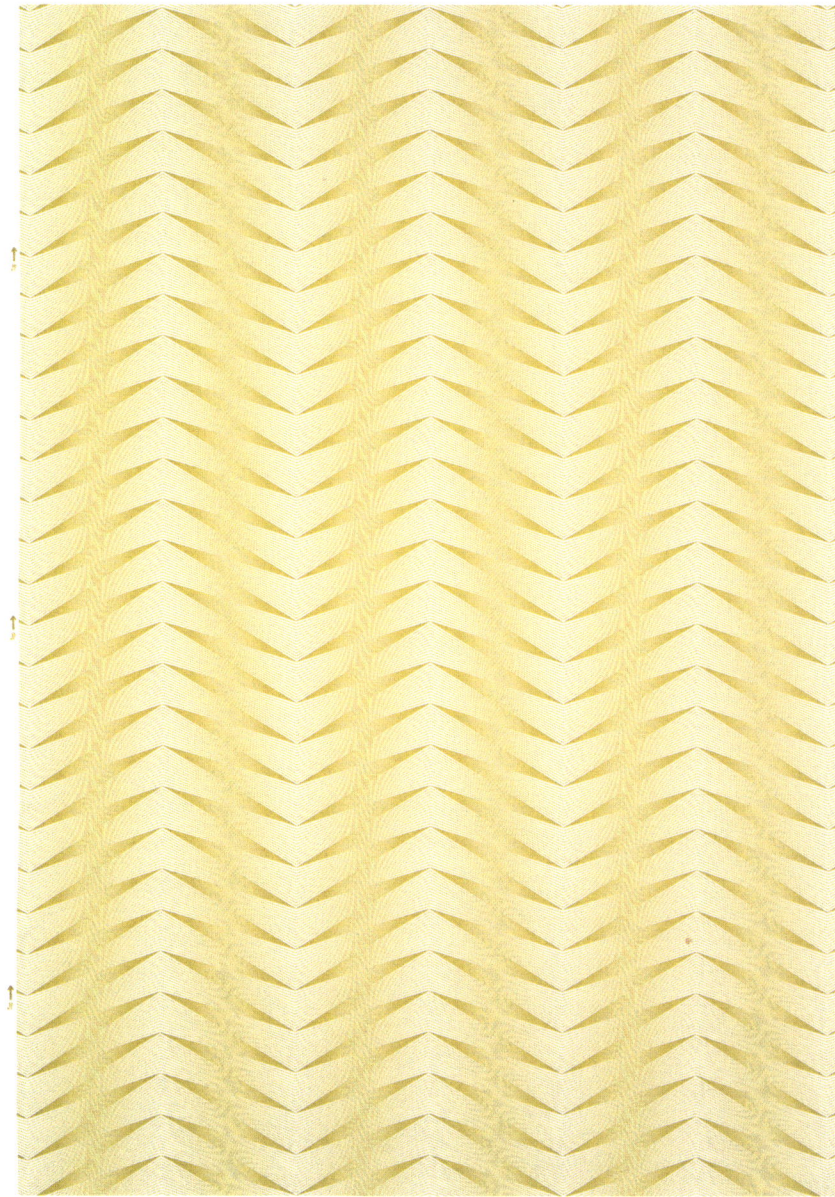

**Helle Graabæk**
(b.1962)

**'Nexus'**
for Kvadrat
Trevira, circa 2002

Helle Graabæk created this design
by hand in order to achieve a varied
expression. Her intention was to
develop ornamentation with a graphic
expression, in which the varied
spacing of the lines give the impression
that there are several colour shades.
The museum acquired the prototype.

Representing several generations, these eight textile
printers have extensive experience with the artistic
and technical process as well as with exhibition and
communication. They want to remind us that experimentation within the field helps develop the craft
and may lead to new aesthetic, technical and material
qualities. Their goal is to bring new energy and dyna-
mism to the field, whether it is practised as design,
craft or art. The hope is to restore the significant position that the craft of textile printing enjoyed from the
1930s to the 1970s.

Designmuseum Danmark's collection is full of
surprises. The one hundred years, roughly speaking,
that the collection spans covers the full spectrum of
printing technology, especially the methods that were
used in the solo studios, such as block printing and
printing screens. Several textile printers also taught
at the School of Arts and Crafts in Copenhagen and
thus influenced the following generations of printers.

During the late 1970s, the Copenhagen school –
which by then had been renamed the School of Decorative Art – took on a new teacher: Joy Boutrup, who
had trained as a textile engineer abroad. She had an
important influence on her students and continues to
be a source of support for some of today's active textile printers. Joy Boutrup had a number of specialized
techniques reintroduced at the school, and with this
skilled and knowledgeable specialist at their side, the
students began to take a more experimental approach
to explore the chemical effects of different forms of
printing. Her excellent communication skills and always inspiring, encouraging and enthusiastic demean-
our make her a pivotal figure, and many students and
active textile printers, both in Denmark and abroad,
have much to thank Joy Boutrup for.

The Danish textile printing culture rests on a strong
studio tradition, in part because the textile industry
was never very big in Denmark. Collaboration between
industry and textile printers in Denmark flourished
for the two or three decades after the war. Many
textile printers produced their textiles in their own
workshops. The incentive for experimenting printing
methods was far greater for someone who was hands-
on throughout the process, from the initial sketch to

the finished piece, than for someone who created a design for an industrial company, which involved handing over the finished drawing and leaving the actual printing to trained textile printers.

Technological innovation also inspired experimentation, as did economic constraints and the need to optimize the utilization of materials and labour. It is important to acknowledge that textile printing is a physically demanding task that requires in-depth knowledge of the craft and chemical processes involved.

The popularity of patterned printed textiles has had its ups and downs over the past 100 years, and even though there have been periods when the modernists did not regard printed textiles as sufficiently pragmatic, time has proven that it is not possible to suppress the joyful and playful use of patterns and colours in home design and clothing culture.

**Charlotte Houman**
(b.1963)

**'Arcos'**
Cotton, 2001

Charlotte Houman graduated from the Danish Design School in 1991. For the *Arcos* exhibition at the Museum of Decorative Art in 2001, she printed textiles using a burn paste and heat. These ideas led to a collaboration on industrial curtains with the curtain company Faber.

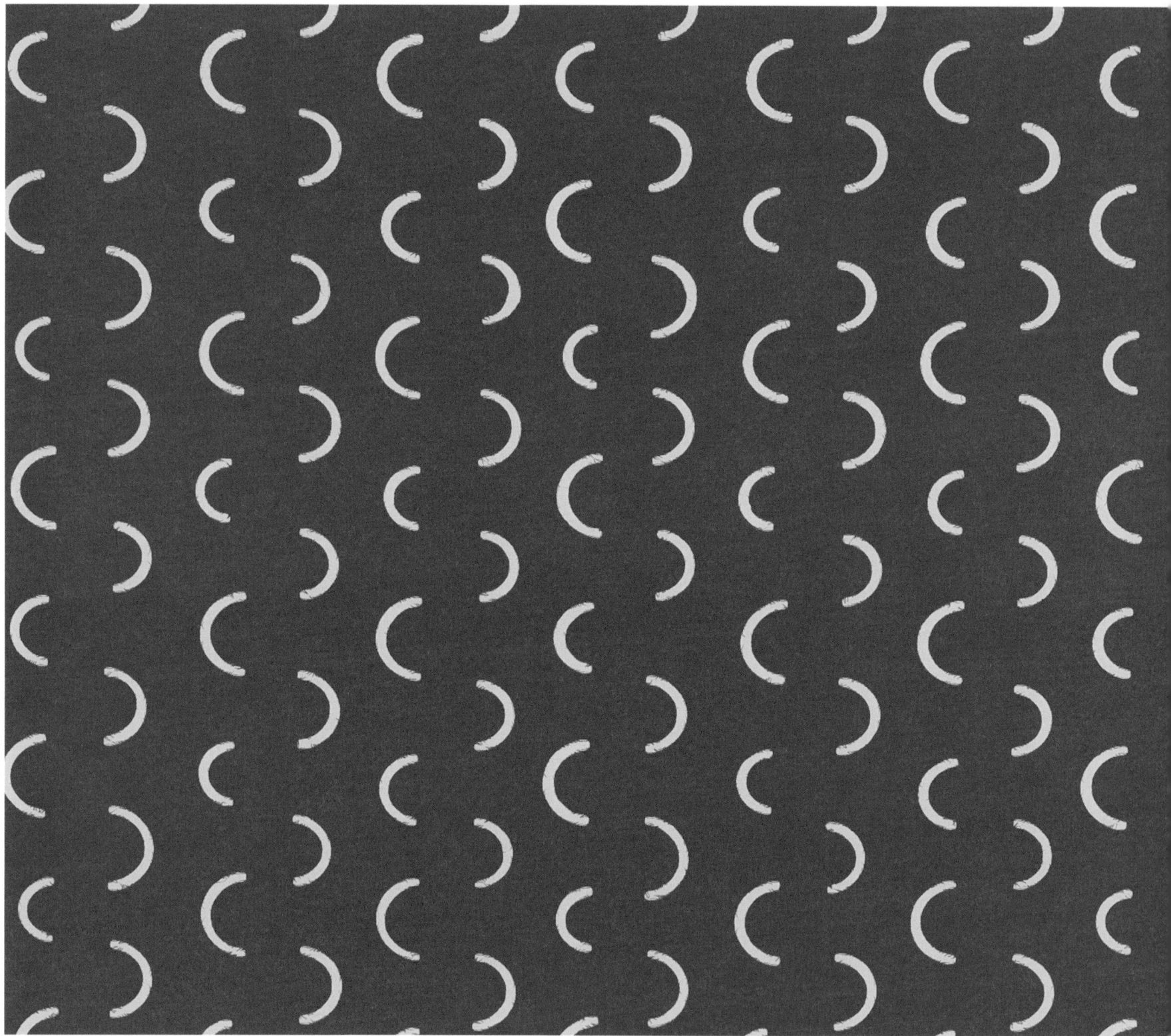

**Lisbet Friis**
(b.1957)

**'Big Flower'**
Linen, 2012

Lisbet Friis (b.1957) makes a living
designing and printing yard goods for
furnishing fabrics but also creates one-
off hand-printed textiles. In order to
make her designs available to a wider
audience, she has her prints produced
abroad.

**Dorte Østergaard Jakobsen**
(b.1957)

**Length of fabric**
Linen, 1992

Dorte Østergaard Jakobsen graduated
from the School of Arts and Crafts
in Copenhagen in 1984. This textile,
which she created after a study stay in
Skagen, was included in the exhibition
*Sand, Stol med Kjole* (Sand, Chair with
Dress) in 1992.

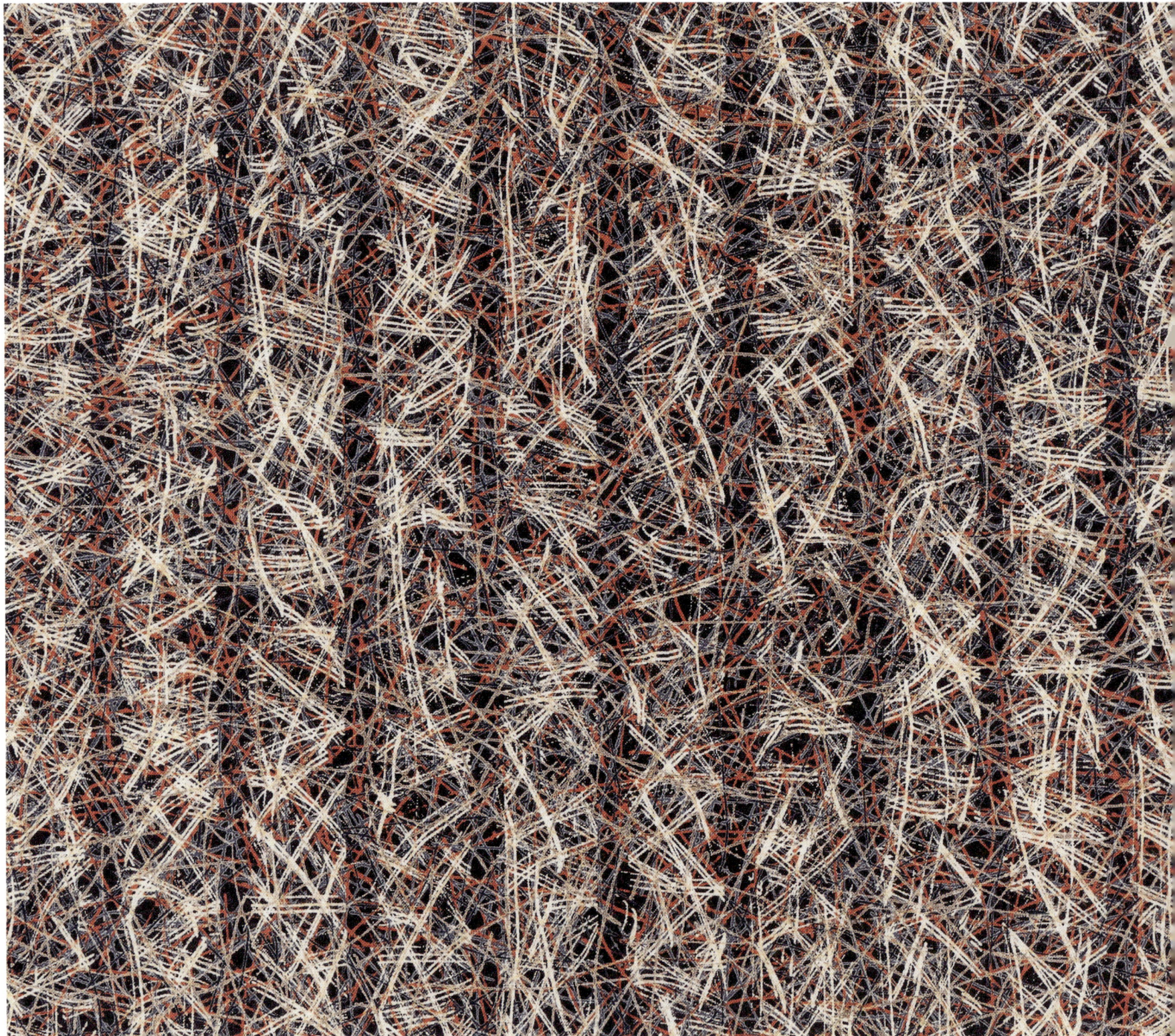

**Louise Sass**
(b.1965)

**'Lineær stak' / 'Linear Stack'**
Cotton, 1995

Louise Sass is one of the most prolific and successful textile printers in Danish design. Like several other contemporary Danish textile printers, printing is not just a craft to her but rather an artistic process, in which colours, shapes, lights and techniques are subjected to ongoing exploration.

**Anne Fabricius Møller**
(b.1959)

**'To Trykker Krohn'**
**/ 'Two Printers Print Krohn'**
Linen, 2001

Like Ruth Hull, Anne Fabricius
Møller explores non-conventional
printing methods. This print was
created in a free-hand drawing
process using a utensil or vessel
containing the thickened ink.

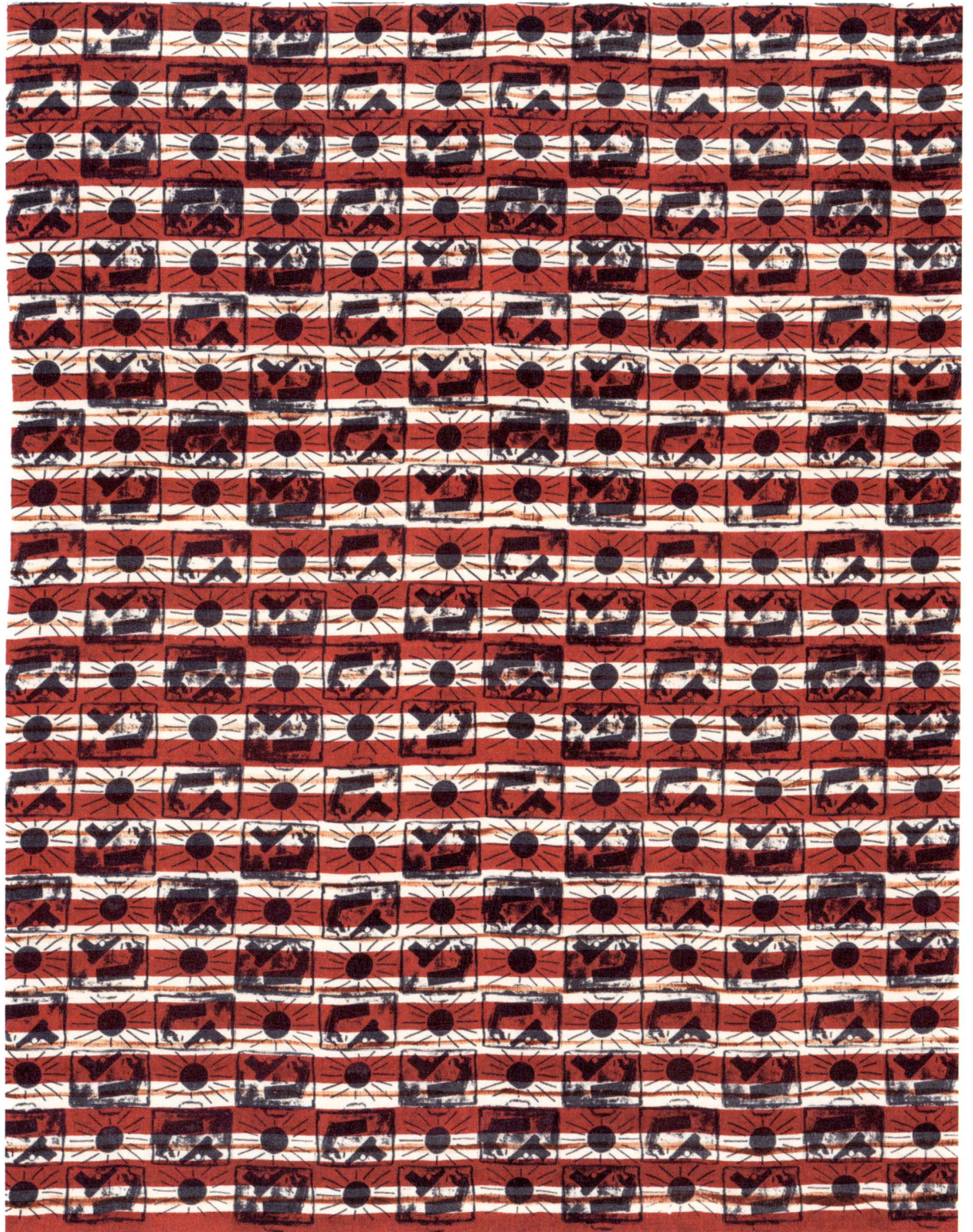

**Vibeke Rohland**
(b.1957)

**'Sunshine in Transit'**
Linen, 1990

Vibeke Rohland's patterns have a
graphic and conceptual expression.
She uses signs and symbols as motifs.
During the time when 'Sunshine in
Transit' was designed, she worked with
X-ray images – here, a packed suitcase.
Juxtaposed with the contents of the
suitcase, the sun with its rays suddenly
takes on different meaning.

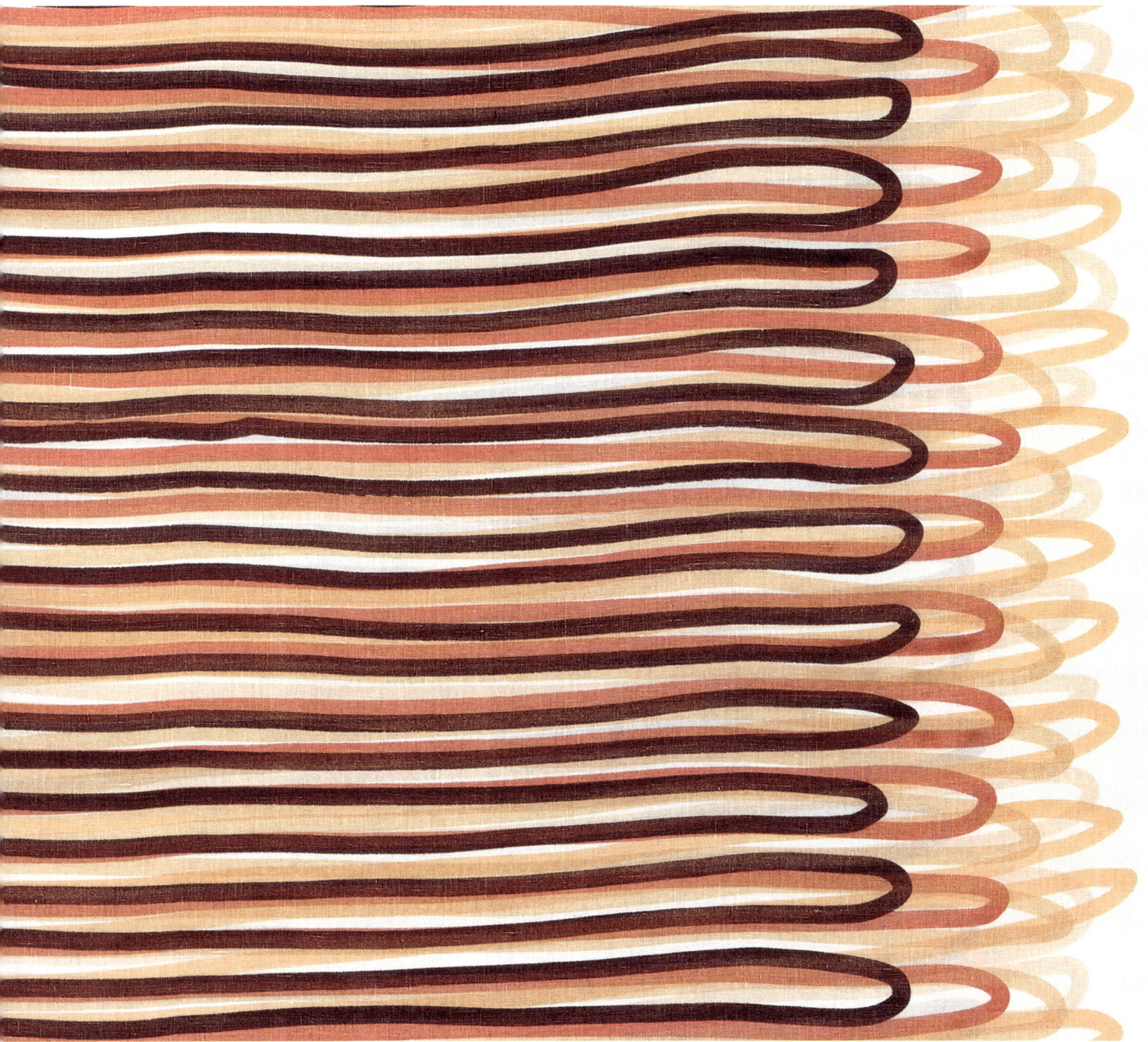

**Vibeke Rohland**
(b.1957)

**'Erasure'**
Velvet, 2019–2021

For her 'Erasure' print, Vibeke Rohland
used layered etching on a dyed piece of
velvet from the manufacturer Kvadrat.

**Else Borup Kallesøe**
(b.1949)

**'Flying Palette'**
Silk organza, 1986

After one year at Aarhus Academy of
Fine Arts, Else Kallesøe studied at the
School of Arts and Crafts in Copenhagen from 1971 to 1976. In 1977, she
spent some time at the Pratt Institute,
School of Art and Design, in New York.
In the 1980s, Else Kallesøe had an
exhibition in the Birger Christensen
fur salon on Østergade, where her
textiles were displayed to passers-by
on this pedestrianized street in central
Copenhagen.

**Margrethe Odgaard**
(b.1978)

**Tablecloth 'Fold – Unfold'**
Cotton, 2010

This tablecloth design was inspired
by a folded tablecloth that developed
yellowish/brown discolouring while
it was kept in a closet for a long time.
The print is mirrored on both axes.
The digitally printed tablecloth is the
prototype for an industrially produced
tablecloth made by Hay.

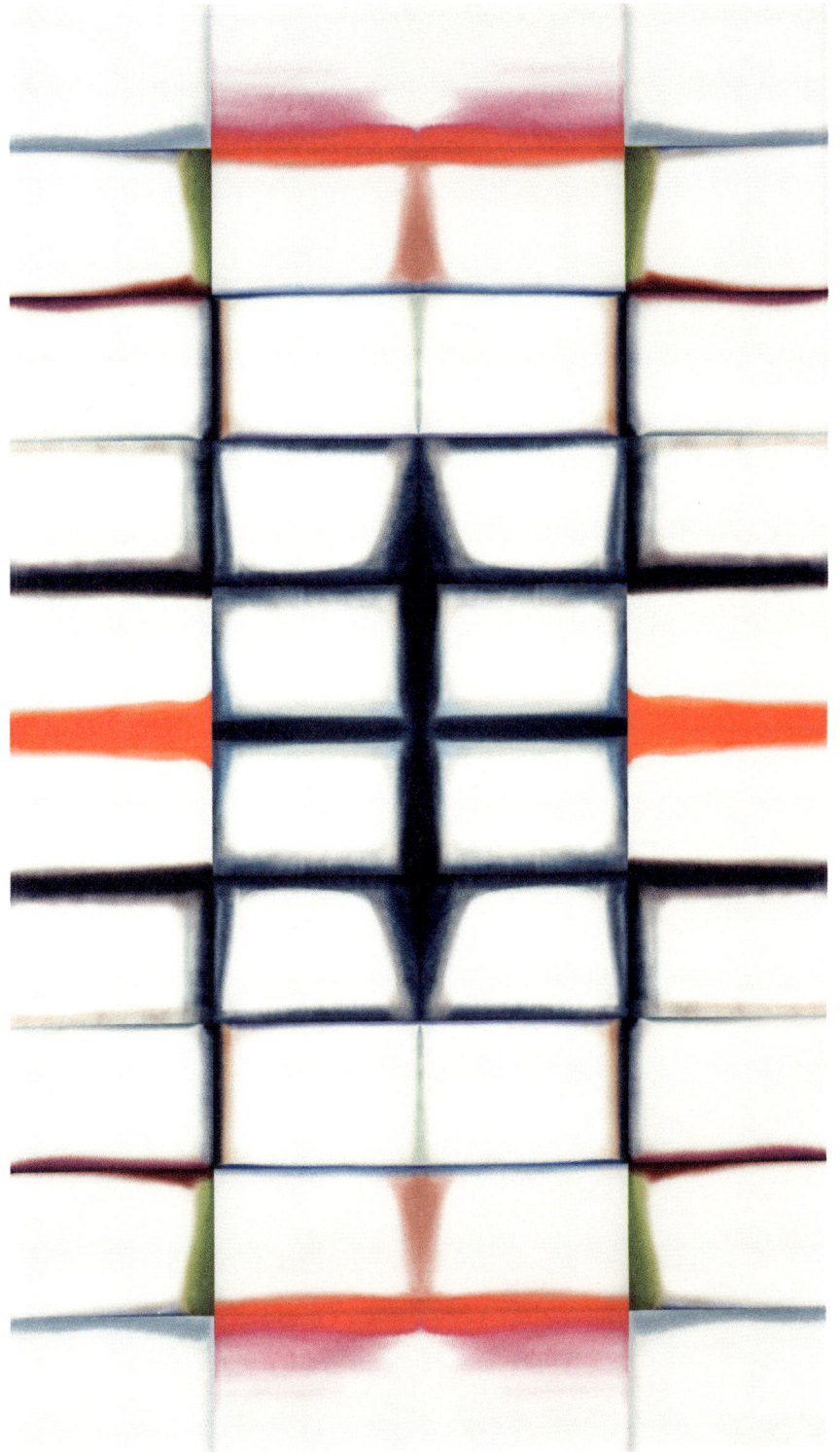

**Louise Sass**
(b.1965)

**'Panorama #1'**
Cotton, 2006

This textile – a hand-painted wall
frieze for a stage curtain – was created
for a decorative project in 2004 at the
nursing home Serafens Äldreboende
in Stockholm.

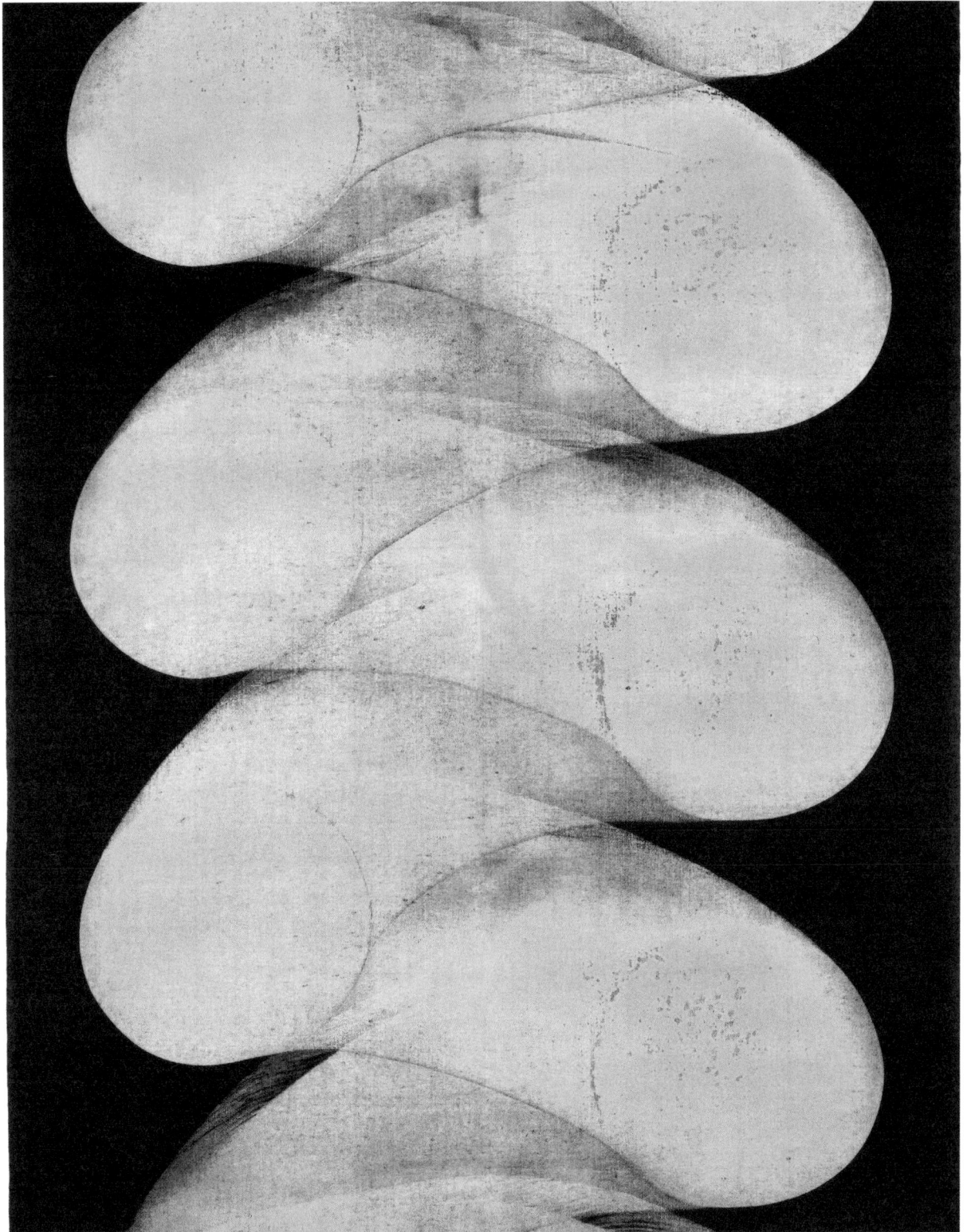

193

**Anne Fabricius Møller**
(b.1959)

**'Igor Krohns bensamling'**
**/ 'Igor Krohn's Bone Collection'**
Linen, 2004

**Nina Ferlov**
(b.1945)

**'Tulipan' / 'Tulip'**
Silk, 1995

Nina Ferlov attended Skals Hånd-
arbejdsskole (Skals Textile Craft
School) in 1965 and graduated
from the School of Arts and Crafts
in Copenhagen in 1969. She did an
internship with Ruth Hull. Nina Ferlov
creates one-off pieces on silks but has
also designed yard goods for Kvadrat.

**Thea Bjerg**
(b.1960)

**'Blå tændrør' / 'Blue Spark Plugs'**
Silk, polyester, 1995–2002

Thea Bjerg graduated from the School
of Arts and Crafts in Copenhagen and
established her own studio in 1987.
A key aspect of her work is the use
of three-dimensional effects in silk
textiles, for example hand-pleated
folds in luxurious shawls or a form
of 'body sculptures'.

**Pernille Holm**
(b.1963)

**Dress-making fabric**
Silk/polyester, 2013

As a textile printer, Pernille Holm has
explored three-dimensional special
techniques. Her textiles are used
for couture, haute couture, stage
productions and industrial design.

**Vibeke Riisberg**
(b.1951)

**'Illusion no. 5'**
Cotton, 1993

This length of fabric was presented
in the exhibition *7 Illusions* at the
Museum of Decorative Art in 1993.
Along with the other textiles in the
exhibition, this hand-printed fabric
formed a proposal for a collaboration
with Kvadrat.

# Index

**Danish Textile Prints: 100 Years of Craft and Design**
© 2025 Kirsten Toftegaard and Strandberg Publishing

Editing: Nicholas Jungblut
Project management: Louise Haslund-Christensen
Translation: Dorte Herholdt Silver
Copyediting: Cornelius Holck Colding
Graphic design: Rasmus Koch Studio
Cover illustration: 'Kirsebær' (Cherries) by Marie
Gudme Leth, 'Profiler' (Profiles) by Inge Ingetoft and
'Digitalis' by Dorte Raaschou, photos: Pernille Klemp
Set in Kepler Std, Flexibility
Paper: Munken Print White
Photo editing: Narayana Press
Printing: Livonia Print

Printed in Latvia, 2025
First edition, first print run
ISBN 978-87-92894-07-6

Strandberg Publishing
Klareboderne 3
DK-1115 Copenhagen
www.strandbergpublishing.dk
mail@strandbergpublishing.dk

A part of the Gyldendal Group

## Illustrations

All illustrations are the property of
Designmuseum Danmark / Photos: Pernille Klemp,
except for the following:

Allan Moe / Ritzau Scanpix – p. 97
Erik Gleie / Ritzau Scanpix – p. 37
Karin Munk – p. 101
Royal Danish Library – pp. 45, 83
Scan from *Dansk Kunsthaandværk* (Danish Crafts), vol. 35,
1962 – pp. 43, 63, 67, 71, 77, 87, 91
Scan from *Gudrun Krabbe: Indtryk på stof og i billeder*
(Gudrun Krabbe: Impressions on textile and in images),
2000 – p. 51

© Anne Fabricius Møller / VISDA
© Arne L. Hansen / VISDA
© Axel Salto / VISDA
© Bitten Hegelund / VISDA
© Dorte Østergaard Jakobsen / VISDA
© Ebbe Sadolin / VISDA
© Egill Jacobsen / VISDA
© Inge Ingetoft / VISDA
© Lisette Kampmann / VISDA
© Louise Sass / VISDA
© Mogens Andersen / VISDA
© Ole Schwalbe / VISDA
© Rolf Middelboe / VISDA
© Ruth Christensen / VISDA
© Stig Lindberg / VISDA
© Verner Panton / VISDA
© Vibeke Riisberg / VISDA

The editors have attempted to identify all the license holders
for the illustrations used in this publication. If we have
missed any, we kindly ask you to contact us, and you will
receive the standard fee.

Published with the generous support of:

**K:**
Danish Arts
Foundation

**AUGUSTINUS FONDEN**
STIFTET 25. MARTS 1942

**Grosserer L.F. Foghts Fond**

**AAGE OG JOHANNE
LOUIS-HANSENS
FOND**

## About the author

Kirsten Toftegaard (b.1951) is trained as a graphic artist and
textile designer from the School of Decorative Art, now the
Royal Danish Academy, and holds an MA in History from the
universities of Copenhagen and Uppsala. Since 1997, she has
worked at the textile and dress collection at Designmuseum
Danmark, where she has curated several major exhibitions,
including *Marimekko – The Story of a Nordic Brand* in 2007,
*Rokoko-mania* in 2012, *Post-war British Textiles* in 2013,
*Mode & Tekstil / Fashion & Fabric* in 2014, *Marie Gudme Leth
– Pioneer of Print* in 2016, *I am Black Velvet: Erik Mortensen
Haute Couture* in 2017, *The Power of Pattern* in 2022 and
*The Power of Print – Danish Textile Prints Through 100 Years.*
Kirsten Toftegaard has published numerous articles on
textiles and fashion in 20th-century Denmark and is the
author of the book *Marie Gudme Leth – en pioner i dansk
stoftryk* (Marie Gudme Leth – A Pioneer in Danish Textile
Printing) from 2021.